THE BELIEVER'S BATTLE STRATEGY

FIGHT FOR THE LIFE CHRIST DIED TO GIVE

CHRISTIE PUNCH MICHAUD

ISBN-13: 978-1-7325589-0-8

Except where otherwise indicated, all Scripture quotations in this book are taken from The ESV® Bible (The Holy Bible, English Standard Version®), copyright © 2001 by Crossway, a publishing ministry of Good News Publishers. Used by permission. All rights reserved.

Scripture marked NLT are taken from the HOLY BIBLE, NEW LIVING TRANSLATION (NLT): Copyright© 1996, 2004, 2007 by Tyndale House Foundation. Used by permission of Tyndale House Publishers, Inc., Carol Stream, Illinois 60188.

Scripture marked NIV are taken from the HOLY BIBLE, NEW INTERNATIONAL VERSION®. NIV®. Copyright © 1973, 1978, 1984 by International Bible Society. Used by permission of Zondervan. All rights reserved worldwide.

Scripture marked MSG are taken from THE MESSAGE, copyright © 1993, 1994, 1995, 1996, 2000, 2001, 2002 by Eugene H. Peterson. Used by permission of NavPress. All rights reserved. Represented by Tyndale House Publishers, Inc. All rights reserved. Used by permission.

Scripture marked AMP are taken from the AMPLIFIED BIBLE (AMP): Scripture taken from the AMPLIFIED® BIBLE, Copyright © 1954, 1958, 1962, 1964, 1965, 1987 by the Lockman Foundation Used by Permission. (www.Lockman.org)

Scripture marked NKJV are taken from the New King James Version. Copyright © 1982 by Thomas Nelson, Inc. Used by permission. All rights reserved.

❀ Created with Vellum

PRAISE FOR THE BELIEVER'S BATTLE STRATEGY

Christie has written a powerful and practical book to help us defeat the enemy of our souls. She shows us the way to stop living beneath our privilege and to embrace the fight for freedom that is ours in Christ.

— DARRIN PATRICK, THE DUDES GUIDE TO MARRIAGE

Christie has a heart for those on the front lines of trouble in their lives. Her new book, *The Believer's Battle Strategy*, is a testament to the absolute power of Jesus Christ in the lives of the hurting, overwhelmed, grief stricken and disillusioned. Every Christian should develop their own Believers Battle Strategy and this book will show you how.

— STEPHANIE HAYNES, CULTIVATING PEACE: RECEIVING GOD'S PEACE WITHIN YOUR CHAOS.

The practical strategies outlined in this book will transform your life and unleash the warrior within.

— CATHY MART, PMHNP, BC, HAVEN CHRISTIAN COUNSELING

Walking through *The Believer's Battle Strategy* in community added a refreshing newness to my lifelong faith, and showed me how to use God's Word to address my biggest challenges. This is not 'just another Bible study or Christian book'; it is a strategy for living life the way God intended.

— SHAUNA ROWLAND, CLASS PARTICIPANT

*I have written to you who are God's children
because you know the Father. I have written to you
who are mature in the faith because you know Christ,
who existed from the beginning. I have written to you
who are young in the faith because you are strong.*

*God's word lives in your hearts,
and you have won your battle with the evil one.*

— 1 JOHN 2:14-15 NLT

TABLE OF CONTENTS

1

THE BATTLE

Fight the good fight for the true faith.

— 1 Timothy 6:12a, NLT

Togo, West Africa 2011

The heat was intense. I sat at a makeshift medical clinic in a foreign land, under the few trees I could find for shade. This was my second time experiencing life among the Togolese people. Although my medical background extended only to administering liquid Tylenol to my young children, my heart was willing to serve. And I did by reviewing medications and instructions with patients before they left the clinic. With flip-flopped feet caked in dirt and sweat soaking through my scrubs, I questioned what help I was really offering.

A petite young woman sat down at my medical station. Her name was Akoua. Her baby sat contently on her back, wrapped in fabric typical of her culture. I reviewed her chart and saw the words "depressed" and "going mad" written in blue ink. As I looked up into her brown eyes, I recognized that quiet desperation.

There are few defining moments in life. For me, this was one. You see, I too battled with depression. Yet, I hid my struggles because *I'm a Christian. I'm supposed to have it all together.* Or so I thought. While depression has its stigma back in the United States, it is nothing like in Togo. I heard God whisper, "You need to tell her you deal with this." He presented me with a choice that would alter the trajectory of my life.

Obediently, I opened up to Akoua through a translator and shared for the first time my similar struggles and what God had been teaching me. As I spoke, relief and hope flooded Akoua's face. Her expression is forever etched in my mind. She realized she was no longer alone. Despite our differences, we were now in the trenches together, fighting similar battles.

The following day, Akoua walked for hours to other villages, looking for me at our new clinic site. It wasn't me drawing her there; it was Truth. We talked about the universal battle we all find ourselves in, and how we are to fight for the life Christ died to give. We parted that day as sisters in Christ, equipped for battle using the Word of God as our ammunition.

When I flew home days later, God made it clear He wasn't through with me as He again whispered, "Now go home and do this." While I didn't know what all "this" would entail, I knew I needed to obey and take humble steps of faith. Since that day, He has taken me on an extraordinary journey of self-discovery, revealing His eye-opening Truth and healing power that can overcome any struggle.

That meeting in Togo was an appointment set up by the Author and Creator of life. This divinely orchestrated moment was not just about two people dealing with depression.

It was a revelation and the birth of a mission:
to see the Truth in any struggle we face.

We all have a story

Our situations, circumstances, belief systems and backgrounds have uniquely shaped who we are today. Yet, as with Akoua and I, our stories are often more similar than they first appear. However, if we are distracted by the noise of the world and not looking for it; we will miss the common thread we all share.

Heartbreak. A wrong choice. Victimization. A bad start. No matter what you've done, been through, or are currently facing, your story is NOT a tragedy. It is a love story—one intertwined with the greatest story ever told. *His story.* Your Heavenly Father loves you so much that He was willing to sacrifice His Son, Jesus, so you could have a happily ever after. Not just when you die, but right now!

Are you only seeing half of yours?

A slight tweak to your life lenses can change its trajectory. There is no struggle too big God cannot miraculously use for good. Think back on your life or even just today.

- Are you suffering a loss you can't get past?
- Have you been betrayed or hurt by someone close and just can't forgive?
- Are you dealing with a sin, secret or addiction that is tearing you apart?

I'm only skimming the surface of struggles you may have experienced. Regardless, are you able to keep your peace and joy in the midst of struggle?

You see, it didn't matter that Akoua and I lived on opposite sides of the globe and had our own unique situations. We were blinded by the same enemy and deceived in similar ways, causing us to fight the same thing: ourselves.

A simple *change in perspective* showed us we had the same Hero, Jesus, walking alongside us at all times.

A simple *shift in strategy* revealed we had all we needed to be victorious in battle.

What are you fighting?

For so long, my past was overshadowed and limited by what I could physically see. I focused on my shortcomings and constantly battled against myself to overcome and become "better." I was often consumed with all the ways I wanted to "improve" for Jesus that it distracted me from *being* and *shining* for Him. While I've come a long way, these struggles still resurface if I do not remain on guard.

If your story is similar to mine, your intentions are good, but most of your days are full of sweat, tears—and let's be honest, a whole lot of condemnation. Am I right? You feel defeated, confused and frustrated because even though you know Christ is in you, you still feel as though you are held captive by something. Why is change not happening? It can leave you feeling guilty, ashamed and … *heavy*.

If this is you, look closer.
Your fight is not with *yourself*.

Maybe you allow what others say or do to determine your happiness. Maybe you're consumed with suspicion, hurt or anger toward someone, or people in general. Do you spend most of your day replaying in your mind the hurtful actions and words of others or what you'd like to say back to them if given the opportunity? If so, your days are most likely filled with a lot of offense, hurt and a desire to control relationships. It can leave you feeling distressed, bitter, judgmental and again … *heavy*.

If this is you, look closer.
Your fight is not with *other people*.

Do you allow your circumstances to determine your mood? Maybe the circumstances you're facing are getting the best of you and you don't see a way out. Just when you think you've overcome a problem, another obstacle surfaces. It can leave you feeling discouraged, afraid, overwhelmed and again ... *heavy.*

If this is you, look closer.
Your fight is not with your *circumstances.*

For we are not fighting against flesh-and-blood enemies, but against evil rulers and authorities of the unseen world, against mighty powers in this dark world, and against evil spirits in the heavenly places (Ephesians 6:12, NLT).

The Bible says we cannot see what we are fighting, thus eliminates yourself, others and circumstances as the real enemy. This is Truth. Take it seriously. We have an unseen enemy determined to keep us focused on our imperfections and sins, the people who hurt us, and our seemingly impossible circumstances. He wants us focused on counterfeits we can see, so we never notice him working strategically behind the scenes. And he's an expert.

The Believer's Battle Strategy shifts our worldly perspectives back to the Word.

The believer's battle is real and universal. Christians all over the world are fighting in the same war against the same rival. But the story doesn't end there. According to John 16:33, we will face many trials and sorrows in this life, but take heart, Jesus, our Lord and Savior, has overcome the world!

Even though we will walk through daily battles until Christ returns, the war—your war—has already been won!

The enemy has been defeated. Through Christ, we've been given more than enough power to be victorious in life. Through the Bible, we've been given the Word of God—our undefeatable weapon! These are God's gifts given to His children, believers all over the world.

> Learn to use your weapon affectively
> and live the way we were meant to—free.

The Believer's Battle Strategy is a spiritual boot camp.

A soldier goes through boot camp to train for his mission. Like it or not, we are soldiers in this battle. Whether you are a veteran or new to the faith, continuous Truth tightening is vital. God is raising up His army and He is calling you to fight for the life Christ died to give.

Boot camps can be intense, but life-changing. As with military training and more recently in new exercise regimens, boot camps require a commitment and lifestyle change. Sure, it's rigorous and can feel overwhelming, but there's a purpose. Boot camps build character, strength and perseverance.

When I asked a Navy veteran about her experience in military training, she shared this with me. "Boot camp was about breaking us so they could make us. As soon as we arrived at camp we had to rid ourselves of civilian life, learn that we were not in control, and that we had no choice but to listen to our superior officers."

As I listened, I saw a parallel to the Christian life. We all have a point where we realize we are broken, not in control, and must listen to our Superior Officer. Military boot camp lasts a couple of months, but spiritual boot camp is a longer process. Growing in humility and remaining teachable are necessary for spiritual growth. As we continue to mature in Christ, we rid ourselves of the world—civilian life.

> Humble yourselves before the Lord
> by training for your mission.

The Believer's Battle Strategy is a life manual to keep on hand.

Building a foundation is a necessary part of training. Only when we understand the *who, what,* and *why;* can we successfully step out and accomplish the *how.* In this manual, we will build on our foundation and learn how to:

- Uncover the real battle and the role we play in it.
- Recognize obstacles that personally keep us from battling effectively.
- Fight victoriously through strategy.
- Live by what is true instead of what we feel.
- Trust God in the battle.

Soldiers don't go through boot camp just to cram for one event and then forget what they've learned. The intent is a change in life-style. When a soldier leaves camp and steps onto the field, he practices what he has learned.

> Keep your manual on hand and be reminded
> to fight like you've trained.

The Believer's Battle Strategy is strategy living.

There are amazing books and sermons on how to grow spiritually. I've read and heard many. But what I've learned answers the mystery of why change often doesn't come. If I don't apply what I've heard or read, I will not learn it. If I don't keep applying what I've learned, I will not maintain it. We are creatures of habit with good intentions but unfortunately become distracted by what we see and forget what we cannot see.

Action is needed for success. Practicing strategy brings life change. Don't just be a part-time student of God's Word, make a career of practicing it. Continually train and form habits of applying God's Word so life-giving actions become second nature.

James 1:22 says *But be doers of the word, and not hearers only, deceiving yourselves.* The *Battle Orders* section at the end of each chapter will help you do this, as it leads you through personal reflection and equips you with new tools to put into practice.

Stay the course, pace yourself, apply
what you learn and trust the process!

The Believer's Battle Strategy is most effective when done in community.

Boot camps are done corporately because of the spiritual, emotional and physical intensity of training. Ask someone who has served in the military. There is a special camaraderie with those who have trained and fought together.

There is strength in numbers. Spiritually speaking, a believer's community would be their church. Just like the military is sectioned into groups, like platoons or bunkers, believers would also benefit from small group settings.

In biblical times, armor bearers acted as aides to their fighting companions. In modern times, specifically with the U.S. Army, a battle buddy is a partner or soldier assigned to assist another soldier in and out of combat. This relationship offers community, encouragement, and accountability.

The *battle buddy* concept provides soldiers with a close relationship to help recognize negative thoughts or feelings, as well as intervene when bad decisions are being made. Sounds like we could all use a battle buddy in this spiritual battle!

Proverbs 27:17 (NIV) says *As iron sharpens iron, so one person sharpens another.* I've learned I need people in my life who know me and who have permission to intervene. I need my battle buddies. They encourage and impart wisdom when I cannot see, call me out when I am in sin, and challenge me when I am being deceived. We all need a second set of spiritual eyes focused on God and what's best for us so we stay the course when life gets tough.

Walking through "spiritual boot camp" in a small group can bring transforming discussions and life-changing results through account-ability. If you do not already have a battle buddy or a bunker group, ask God to reveal them to you. Look within your church family, biological family, friends and neighbors. Seek out these life-giving relationships and consider asking them to join you on this journey.

Always remember, you are never alone in this fight! John 14:16 says you have a Constant Helper who is there to comfort, advocate, intercede, and strengthen you. The Holy Spirit is your number one battle buddy who never leaves your side and is incapable of letting you down.

Step out in community and start winning the battle!

Conclusion

Therefore, we are ambassadors for Christ, God making his appeal through us. We implore you on behalf of Christ, be reconciled to God (2 Corinthians 5:20).

As Christians, we have joined God's army. We are also His adopted children with an inheritance beyond measure. Each of us plays an integral part in the battle. God has provided us with more power than we could ever ask for or imagine. The *Believer's Battle Strategy* will equip you with practical tools to fight so you can stand your ground in victory and win the daily battle.

Will you take this step of faith? I join the apostle Paul in praying Ephesians 1:17-19b (NIV), *that the God of our Lord Jesus Christ, the glorious Father, may give you the Spirit of wisdom and revelation, so that you may know him better. I pray that the eyes of your heart may be enlight-ened in order that you may know the hope to which he has called you, the riches of his glorious inheritance in his holy people, and his incomparably great power for us who believe.*

BATTLE ORDERS
Ch 1 - The Battle

Since God's Word is the basis of this book and the key to winning the battle, please spend a good bit of time reflecting and meditating on His Word every day. Keep a separate journal with you and wrestle out what God is revealing in each chapter before moving forward. Let's seek transformation of the heart, and not just head knowledge.

Each *Battle Orders* section will challenge you to identify take aways, be introspective and learn how to practice a new battle tool.

TAKEAWAYS: Identify and write down three takeaways from this chapter. Share with a friend so they stick.

1.

2.

3.

REFLECTION: Wrestle with the following questions and write out your answers in a separate journal. Then, look up each verse and see if your answers line up with scripture.

1. What does it mean to be a Christ follower? (Matthew 4:19, 16:24)
2. If you were to die today, how sure are you that you would spend eternity in heaven? Why do you believe this? (John 3:16, 14:6; Ephesians 2:8)

3. Complete this statement: "In order to follow Christ, I must …" (Romans 10:10, John 10:27)
4. What is the difference between being a Christian and being a soldier for Christ? (Ephesians 5:11, 6:10-18; Romans 12:1-2)

BATTLE TOOL: Commit

To the Winning Side: Have you accepted Christ as your Savior? If you are reading this book, it is clear God is calling out to you. If you are unsure of your salvation or have never asked Christ to be your Lord and Savior, take the time right now and address it; *because if you acknowledge and confess with your mouth that Jesus is Lord [recognizing His power, authority, and majesty as God], and believe in your heart that God raised Him from the dead, you will be saved* (Romans 10:9, AMP, emphasis mine).

- Recognize and acknowledge your need for your Savior Jesus Christ.
- Confess and repent of your sinful ways.
- Desire a relationship with Jesus and invite Him into your life.

Pray a sinner's prayer like the following:

Heavenly Father, I recognize that I am a sinner in need of Jesus, my Savior. I confess my sins and ask for your forgiveness. Thank you for sending your Son, Jesus, to die on the cross for my sin. I receive His sacrifice and seek to live as He did while He was physically on earth. I recognize that I cannot do any of this without your Holy Spirit living inside of me. God, I invite all of you into my heart and surrender my life today. In Jesus name, Amen

Congratulations! Welcome to the winning side! Now, it's important to tell someone, find a Bible-based church to attend and allow the

Holy Spirit to produce His fruit in you. Find other believers willing to walk alongside you and help you get connected. Seek out believers to aid you on this journey and help you take your next steps.

To Boot camp: God has chosen you. Now it's your turn to accept. Just like a soldier goes through the recruitment process and commits by signing enlistment papers, I challenge you to commit to training. We are in this together, but this commitment is between you and God, your Superior Officer. For accountability, read through, initial and sign each commitment step below. Then, tell someone about this journey and invite them to join you.

_____ I will prayerfully seek out *battle buddies* to walk through training with me. I recognize the need for motivation, encouragement and accountability during this process.

_____ I will not just take this book or others' words for Truth; but will prayerfully take it to the Lord and meditate on His Word for true revelation.

_____ I commit to completing *The Believer's Battle Strategy* no matter how long it takes. I recognize this is not a sprint, but a marathon.

_____ I will reflect on my *Battle Orders* in a separate journal and apply each *Battle Tool* before moving to the next chapter. I understand this is key to learning and maintaining what I learn.

_____ I will trust God throughout the process doing what I know to do and leaving the rest in His more than capable hands.

_____ I will recognize the seriousness of this journey and that there is an enemy trying to keep me from this healing process. I will remain in continual prayer for protection over my mind and heart, and I will choose to persevere by trusting my *Constant Battle Buddy.*

_____ At it's completion, I commit to pursuing strategy maintenance by continuing to fight like I trained.

_____
Signature and Date

2

EYES TO SEE

I pray that the eyes of your heart may be enlightened ...

— EPHESIANS 1:18A, NIV

2014 TOGO, WEST AFRICA - MEDICAL CLINIC DAY 3

I was in charge of the "glasses station." My role consisted of helping patients improve their eyesight by providing a pair of glasses. I stared at the disarray of eyeglasses scattered across the wooden table. There were so many. A few were new reading glasses labeled with the lens power, but the majority were pre-owned far and near-sighted lenses of various strengths.

I'm supposed to help people find the right glasses? How? I have no training, and there are so many...

Looking through each pair, I hoped for the best, fully dependent on my interpreter to communicate with each Togolese patient. At random, I picked out eyeglasses in faith and prayed, "God, you make the impossible possible. Let's see you work!" It didn't happen with the first or second patient, but eventually the miraculous occurred!

An elderly Togolese man stepped up, telling us he'd always been visually impaired. I handed him a pair of eye glasses and then a few others thinkings to myself, *there's no way.* Oh, me of little faith!

Suddenly, the man jumped and planted his feet with arms outstretched and eyes wide open. "I can see!" he yelled, looking amazed. His vision had been clouded the majority of his life, but not anymore. Now, he could see!

This happened many times throughout my clinic days. It's a beautiful picture of how God brings sight to the blind, both physically and spiritually.

Open our Eyes

He will open the eyes of the blind and unplug the ears of the deaf (Isaiah 35:5, NLT).

God brings sight to the blind in Elisha's story, an Old Testament prophet to Israel. In 2 Kings 6, Elisha could already *see* spiritually, but his servant could not. The kingdom of Aram had been at war with Israel. Each time Aram formed a new strategy against the Israelites, Elisha received divine knowledge of their plans. This, of course, enraged the enemy, who then diverted their attention toward Elisha.

Was Elisha afraid? No, because he was looking at his situation through spiritual lenses. His servant, however, was terrified and with good reason, given the physical ramifications of what was bound to happen.

Do not be afraid, for those who are with us are more than those who are with them." Then Elisha prayed and said, "O Lord, please open his eyes that he may see" (2 Kings 6:16-17b).

Elisha interceded in prayer for God to give his servant spiritual sight. As the Lord answered Elisha's prayer, his servant's perspective changed. In fact, this scripture goes on to say the servant now saw hills full of horses and chariots of fire. I'm sure the servant's expression and stance suddenly resembled that of my elderly Togolese patient.

What Elisha's servant saw was not a new physical army of Israel, but a much stronger spiritual army few can see but is very real. The servant who once felt powerless now saw God's great heavenly army, who had been there all along.

Like Elisha's servant, in a spiritual sense, we need to recognize our visual deficiencies. We need our eyes to be opened to the battle and prayer plays a big part. In the New Testament, the apostle Paul prayed this similar "spiritual eye-opening" prayer for the Ephesians.

I pray that the eyes of your heart may be enlightened in order that you may know the hope to which he has called you, the riches of his glorious inheritance in his holy people, and his incomparably great power for us who believe (Ephesians 1:18-19a, NIV).

Paul's audience already knew Jesus and His miraculous sacrifice, but their eyes and hearts still had deficiencies. Like the Ephesians, we need spiritual lenses to continually see the following:

- The spiritual battle
- The whole story – His story
- The real enemy and his plans against us
- The believer's mission

How do we see spiritually? Hebrews 12:2 says our eyes need to be *looking to Jesus, the founder and perfecter of our faith*. But, how do we do that since Jesus is no longer physically walking this earth, and now resides at the right hand of God the Father?

Mankind is both physical and spiritual.

*So God created man in his own image, in the image of God he created him;
male and female he created them* (Genesis 1:27).

When God physically created man, He spiritually breathed life into him. When Adam and Eve disobeyed, they were still physically alive, but a spiritual death occurred. When Jesus was crucified, rose from the dead and ascended into heaven; His followers were spiritually reborn.

What this means is that mankind (man and woman) was made in the image of God, making us both physical and spiritual beings. We have a body that sees, breathes, walks and talks. We have a soul that feels and thinks. And we have a spirit that is alive in Christ. We fix our gaze on Christ by looking beyond the physical and seeing life through the eyes of our heart.

Seeing spiritually does not come automatically. It takes belief, intentionality and trust in the One who came and died for us. We have to see and understand who we're fighting so we can win the daily battle and live life to the fullest.

The Spiritual Battle

In my experience, many people have downplayed the spiritual battle or tried to ignore its existence. It's easy to do because you cannot physically "see" it. However, Paul clearly states in Ephesians 6:12 (NIV) what we're really fighting against; *not flesh and blood, but against the rulers, authorities, powers of this dark world and spiritual forces of evil in the heavenly realms.*

We have an intimidating enemy—maybe even an entire army—battling against us that we cannot see. Early on in Paul's life, he persecuted Christians. But on the way to Damascus, he was divinely transformed and made into God's vessel to proclaim the Gospel to all nations. Through Paul's story, God reveals how people are not the real enemy even when they seem to be. Our fight is not against physical or human opponents, but spiritual enemies.

The rulers, authorities, and powers of this dark world...

At first glance, I thought this description referred to people such as biblical-time kings and modern-day authority figures such as government officials, politicians or even police officers. I find it interesting how this very moment, the world is creating a message of hate and corruptness toward those very ones who seek to protect and govern.

What about all the good being done? We rarely hear good news from the media, resulting in a blanket statement of negativity that taints all in each category.

Further study of Ephesians 6:12 reveals spiritual terms such as "cosmic powers, principalities, unseen world" which are clearly not physical. Also, let's not skip over the term "dark" world. Jesus is our Heavenly Father's only begotten Son. Is it just mere coincidence the world's source of physical light is also called the "sun"?

Jesus, the light of the world, became flesh and blood *so that by his death he might break the power of him who holds the power of death—that is the devil* (Hebrews 2:14, NIV). Satan has a spiritual army behind him fighting against Jesus' purposes for us.

... and spiritual forces of evil in the heavenly realms.

There were plenty of kings in the Bible who brought about evil, and there are some authority figures today walking this same path. However, if you look spiritually, you can see they are only a counterfeit or distraction from the Truth. There is a spiritual mastermind behind the scenes using mankind's sin and unwise decisions for his evil purposes. All of this is taking place in a realm we cannot physically see, but is very real.

His Story

With any good story, there is a theme, an antagonist and a hero. There is a beginning, middle and end. And yes, we already know the ending. In John 19:30, the lead role proclaims, *It is finished.* The war has already been won. Therefore, your hero, Jesus, who physically came to earth to defeat death, is your physical and spiritual victor. Your story is about Jesus coming back for you.

That's the CliffsNotes® version. Jesus came not just to save us after we die, but also to give a victorious life so we can shine with radiance and joy *now*, and be a living testimony *now* to a deceived world. He has equipped us with spiritual weapons, so we can fight, and He has deposited the Holy Spirit within all believers, giving us the ability to overcome our flesh and all the power of the evil one. However, in order to fulfill our role, we must be able to recognize and remember His story. *God, open our eyes so that we might see!*

The Beginning

There is so much more to the beginning of His story than the creation of man. In Genesis 1:1, God, who has no beginning, created two different masterpieces; the heavens and the earth. The spiritual and the physical. The seen and the unseen.

With the earth came mankind, billions and counting. But first, with the creation of the heavens, came a multitude of angels who were present at the conception of the world; and whose job as messengers and agents of God was, and still is, to carry out His purposes.

Just like there was a fall of man, there was first a spiritual fall involving God's arch agent of worship. Jesus, the Light, who was there from the beginning, saw Satan fall like lightning from heaven. Herein lies the tragedy.

Lucifer, whose name originally meant "morning star" but soon changed to "adversary", was a mighty angelic guardian established and anointed by his Creator. Unfortunately, he became so prideful in his perfect beauty, he tried to procure God's worship and glory for himself. This evil brought about his fateful demise. The morning star became the prince of darkness and was cast out of heaven.

> *Then war broke out in heaven. Michael and his angels fought against the dragon, and the dragon and his angels fought back...The great dragon was hurled down—that ancient serpent called the devil, or Satan, who leads the whole world astray. He was hurled to the earth, and his angels with him* (Revelation 12:7,8 NIV).

Satan is the enemy, and did you catch that he is not alone? Rulers, authorities, principalities, powers and other spiritual forces of evil are awaiting their orders. A great battle between two spiritual armies is taking place this very moment. Satan and his army of fallen angels continue to oppose God's great army.

Satan is the thief who has come to steal, kill and destroy. When he fell from heaven, he resumed his quest to steal God's glory. However, his focus shifted to God's creation: mankind. Now, he accuses us before God day and night, and distorts our perspectives by planting seeds of doubt.

Satan's whole goal is to distract us from or make us question God and His Word. He wants to keep us from knowing God's promises in our hearts, and he will do anything he can to keep our minds focused on anything other than the Truth that sets us free. Adam and Eve, the first man and woman, were not prepared for Satan's clever tactics. Their choices brought about another fall, which changed humanity forever.

The Middle

At the second fall, mankind's spirit died and sin separated them from God. Only with an innocent lamb sacrificed by a high priest for a specific sin could an individual be made right with God. That is, until his next sin.

When Jesus came to earth and lived a sinless life, He revealed Himself as God. He became both our ultimate Sacrifice and High

Priest by defeating death and fully cleansing those who call on Him as Lord. Through Jesus alone, we become spiritually reborn. He now sits at the right hand of the Father in heaven, clothes believers in His righteousness and intercedes on their behalf.

This is where we find ourselves in His story—the time between man's fall and when Christ returns for His church. John 3:16 states God loves the world and exchanged His son for all who believe. Every man and woman will have the opportunity to choose for themselves what they believe, whom they will serve and where they will spend eternity.

> Satan, who is the god of this world, has blinded the minds of those who don't believe. They are unable to see the glorious light of the Good News. They don't understand this message about the glory of Christ, who is the exact likeness of God (2 Corinthians 4:4, NLT).

Satan's intent is to confuse, dilute or, in a word, "blind" mankind from the good news of the Gospel. Satan wants the unbeliever to remain spiritually dead. If he can do that, there's no need for further attack because they are in essence his allies.

> I will put enmity between you and the woman, and between your offspring and her offspring; he shall bruise your head, and you shall bruise his heel" (Genesis 3:15).

Christ followers, on the other hand, are facing something completely different, an ongoing battle. Satan is furious and seeking revenge, and we are the "offspring" he has come to try and take down. At this very moment, according to Revelation 12:10, he is hurling his arrows of accusation. Why? It's not because of something we did (and we've done plenty). It's because of who we are. Believers, we are cherished by our Creator, our Heavenly Father who finds great pleasure in loving and blessing us. We are His children, His masterpieces, whom He has predestined for His purposes.

Think about it: What is a parent's most prized possession? If you were a villain seeking revenge against someone, whom would you target? His children. We were made in God's image to reflect His glory. This is why the enemy hates us and wants to stifle any sight of God's image within us.

Should we be afraid? Absolutely not! Ultimately, who's in charge—the Creator or the creation? Remember, in the beginning God. Everything was created by Him and for Him (the heavens and the earth, the spiritual and the physical). He is the potter, and we are the clay. He is the beginning and the end, the Alpha and Omega. He is all-powerful, all-knowing and always present. He is the one true God in three persons – Father, Son and Holy Spirit. And He is the author, director, producer and main character of this great story we find ourselves in. We are the supporting cast in this suspenseful drama.

Several believers, including Elisha and Paul, have walked before us, their stories recorded in the Bible for us to learn from. Each was created for a purpose and called to partner in God's mission. We are called to do the same. In the coming chapters, we will discover the ways God works through us, His beloved children.

The End

Because of the Gospel, believers can remain at peace no matter what the future holds. We know how this magnificent story ends, although it is still to come and involves a great final battle. Revelation 20 states Satan will go out and deceive the nations in every corner of the earth. He will gather a mighty army, as numberless as sand along the seashore.

But fire came down from heaven and consumed them, and the devil who had deceived them was thrown into the lake of fire and sulfur where the beast and the false prophet were, and they will be tormented day and night forever and ever (Revelation 20:9b-10).

Is this really the end or just the ending to our enemy
and another great climax to His story that never ends?

One day, Jesus will come down from the clouds for His church and reign in a new heaven and new earth.

Our Role in His story

As the enemy came down toward him, Elisha prayed to the LORD, *"Strike this army with blindness." So, he struck them with blindness, as Elisha had asked* (2 Kings 6:18, NIV).

Ironically, as we're talking about the spiritual opening of believers' eyes, Elisha's story ends with the army of Aram being struck with their own blindness, a physical deficiency. Elisha prayed a bold prayer and the Lord answered. As the greatest story continues to unfold, God wants us to see we are not helpless beings in the midst of this battle. There are two sides in this spiritual battle, two opposing armies, and we have been given the opportunity to be a branch of God's army.

God has invited—not forced, but invited—each of us to play a valuable role in His story. What God intends will ultimately happen regardless of our participation; however, I want to receive the prize of my high calling. I want to experience immeasurable blessings and abundance in this life as I store up treasures for the next. How about you?

Believers, we've been given a mission: the Great Commission.

We can confidently fight in the trenches because:

- We are on the winning side.

Little children, you are from God and have overcome them, for he who is in you is greater than he who is in the world (1 John 4:4).

- Satan's power is limited.

One day the angels came to present themselves before the LORD, *and Satan also came with them... The* LORD *said to Satan, "Very well, then, everything he has is in your power, but on the man himself do not lay a finger." Then Satan went out from the presence of the Lord* (Job 1:6,12, NIV).

- We are protected.

But the Lord is faithful. He will establish you and guard you against the evil one. (2 Thessalonians 3:3).

- Whatever God allows, He will ultimately use for good.

And we know that for those who love God all things work together for good, for those who are called according to his purpose (Romans 8:28).

- Satan's time is running out.

The devil has come down to you in great wrath, because he knows that his time is short! (Revelation 12:12b).

- Satan cannot touch us.

God's Son holds them securely, and the evil one cannot touch them (1 John 5:18b, NLT).

- We already know the ending.

I have said these things to you, that in me you may have peace. In the world you will have tribulation. But take heart; I have overcome the world (John 16:33).

Conclusion

Believers, we are on mission. Are you wearing your spiritual lenses? Can you *see* the vast heavenly army present as you walk out your role in His story? The perfectionist in me wants to force the eyes of my heart open by my best efforts, but it doesn't work that way. God is the author and perfecter of our faith not us, and He is the one who transforms us more into Jesus' image, not us. And He is working this very moment to complete the process.

All He needs from us is a willingness to trust Him and His Word, and to listen and meditate on Truth. God's Word must become more than just head knowledge. In order for us to truly see, God's Word needs to be imprinted on our hearts.

We are on the winning side, and the war has already been won.
Let's accept our role in His story!

BATTLE ORDERS
Ch 2 - Eyes to See

TAKEAWAYS: Identify and write down three takeaways from this chapter. Share with a friend so they stick.

1.

2.

3.

REFLECTION: Wrestle with the following questions. Write out your answers in a separate journal, then discuss for clarity and accountability.

1. What do you believe about the spiritual battle?
2. How does the spiritual realm affect our earthly lives?
3. What mission has God given you in His greater story?
4. What is holding you back from your mission?

BATTLE TOOL: Ask (Pray Scripture)

Our story is intertwined with His story. To fully understand ours, we must see the spiritual side of the story and the parallels that affect our lives daily. There is life-changing importance and victory in *seeing* the whole story.

1. Ask God to open your eyes to the Truth and what is unseen. Pray Psalm 119:18.
2. Confess if there is any doubt, skepticism or confusion to the spiritual battle or our role in it. Pray Mark 9:24.
3. Ask God how He wants you to respond, and what more He wants to reveal. For example, Pray 1 John 5:14 and James 1:5.
4. Pray through scripture cited in this chapter and others that come to mind. For example, Knowing Truth is His will for us in Christ Jesus. Pray John 8:32.

*Go deeper verses from this chapter: Hebrews 2:14, 12:2; Job 38:4-7; Psalm 103:20; Genesis 1:3–4; Luke 1:18; Colossians 1:16; Ezekiel 28:12-17; Romans 8:34; 1 John 5:7-8; Revelation 1:7, 12:17, 21:1; Philippians 1:6, 3:14; 2 Corinthians 3:1.

THE THIEF'S PLAN

The thief comes only to steal and kill and destroy...

— JOHN 10:10A

2006 CHARLESTON, SC

I had everything I thought I wanted—a loyal husband, a precious newborn and a home to call my own. I even lived in the beautiful city of Charleston, SC. Yet, I couldn't escape a hollow and unexplainable weight of sadness.

I lost interest in the things I loved, such as being outside surrounded by God's beauty and the radiance of the sun. I would stand in my foyer, gaze through the storm door glass and be unable to step out. Something was terribly wrong.

I hadn't walked through tragedy like others, so why did I feel this way? I concluded that I was weak. I was the tragedy. I would isolate and seek solace by consuming junk food and watching mindless TV. It didn't work. I couldn't escape the heaviness that gripped my heart. I cried myself to sleep at night, often with my Bible wrapped in my arms.

For months, this secret, paralyzing prison was my reality. This was postpartum depression, yes...but also something more. I realized this captive feeling wasn't new. It was actually very familiar and had been there ever since I could remember—only it was progressively getting worse.

Looking back, I see my destructive patterns. I would hide each time I became tired of pretending I was okay, and then overwhelmed with self-hatred because I was not. I realize now it was God I was actually hiding from as I tried to fill myself with everything but Him. I was too ashamed. I pushed my feelings into the deep crevices of my soul, attempted to forget and stepped back out in my own strength, only to try again.

But not this time. I couldn't pretend anymore. Desperation was written all over my face. The mental abuse had beaten me down and stolen my joy. Focusing only on what I could feel or see killed my hopes and dreams. Wrong thinking was slowly destroying my life.

I don't want to go back to that time in my life, and I don't have to. God has revealed Himself in extraordinary ways since that season.

So much of our lives have been wasted in ways God never intended. Why? Because we have been "blinded" by what we "see."

Understanding the real enemy we are dealing with and his specific plot to take each one of us down is crucial to fighting and winning. John 10:10 says there is a thief who has come to steal, kill and destroy. But we tend to waste all kinds of energy fighting everything but this thief.

Not anymore. The enemy lines have been infiltrated and his crafty plans exposed! All the intelligence we need for victory in this life has been provided for us in God's Word. It's time for the thief's plans—his steal tactics—to be taken down one by one.

The First Attack

Through Adam and Eve's story in Genesis 3, Satan has given us multiple clues to his attack strategy, his steal tactics. Adam was originally given the perfect garden and a true connection to God the Father. Man's purpose was to know and glorify God, and specifically for Adam to tend and watch over the garden. The first thing God told Adam after placing him in Eden was an instruction:

And the Lord God commanded the man, saying, "You may surely eat of every tree of the garden, but of the tree of the knowledge of good and evil you shall not eat, for in the day that you eat of it you shall surely die" (Genesis 2:16-17).

Just like a parent lays out boundaries for their children's good, God did the same here. Man was given complete freedom to do anything *except* one thing, take of the forbidden fruit. He then determined it was not good for man to be alone and thus created woman.

God created the earth and all that is in it in six days. His final masterpiece, man and woman, was the only handiwork He breathed His life into. He looked over all He had made and declared 'it was very good'! This is the point in the story where we'd like to see man and woman ride off into the sunset and live happily ever after.

Unfortunately, in comes the master deceiver...

"The serpent was the shrewdest of all the wild animals the LORD God had made..." (Genesis 3:1a NLT).

The serpent is Satan, the ancient one who has come to deceive the world. In Adam and Eve's story, we can see Satan's plan unfold as he conceals and misrepresents the Truth through subtle steal tactics. Our enemy wants us to remain preoccupied with thinking and believing what is false. The serpent's technique is unseen. It is mental assaults and this deception comes in various forms.

The Doubt Tactic

"...One day he asked the woman, "Did God really say you must not eat the fruit from any of the trees in the garden?" (Genesis 3:1b, NLT).

Who did God give the instruction not to eat from the tree of the knowledge of good and evil? Adam. Remember, Eve wasn't created yet. Who did the serpent target? Eve.

We can assume Adam shared the warning with Eve, because Genesis 3:23 implies she did know it; however, there is no evidence of God giving her this instruction directly. The serpent simply asked a question that he still implies to us today. "Did God really say _____?" Through this questioning, Satan planted his seeds of doubt towards God's instruction, which then fostered uncertainty.

Could it be that doubt or deception came easier to Eve because she didn't receive this instruction directly from God, but from man? Was this why she was the first target, or the easier target?

This was eye-opening for me as the world constantly poses the "Did God really say or mean that?" question. To overcome the doubt tactic, we need a strong foundation and knowledge of the Bible. We need to know what God really says.

God has given us His Word, and according to 2 Timothy 3:16, it's an entire book of His direct instruction. Do not be intimidated. Whether you have grown up reading the Bible or are just starting, God will speak to those who are hungry for His instruction.

Start wherever you are and see the Bible come alive. There are many anointed authors, pastors and speakers out there; but their messages aren't meant to take the place of God's direct messages to us. We must know God's Word for ourselves and not from others' hearsay.

Lesson Learned:
Don't become an easy target. Remain in God's Word
and get to know His instructions directly.

The Distraction Tactic

"You won't die!" the serpent replied to the woman. "God knows that your eyes will be opened as soon as you eat it, and you will be like God, knowing both good and evil" (Genesis 3:4–5, NLT).

Satan contradicted God's instruction and played on man's God-given desire to *see.* Eve listened to Satan's lie. Big mistake! She began to dialogue with the enemy, and confusion set in. This crafty serpent's appeal was to the same type of worldly temptations distracting us today.

For the world offers only a craving for physical pleasure, a craving for everything we see, and pride in our achievements and possessions. These are not from the Father, but are from this world (1 John 2:16, NLT).

PRIDE is the very thing that brought Satan's demise. It's powerful and he wants believers to fall prey to its effects. When pride rises, life becomes all about the individual. I believe the biggest distraction of all is self. We live in an "all about me" world, which the Fall set into motion, our flesh feeds on and the enemy courts. The world tells us to focus on wealth, status, beauty—basically, anything that steals our focus, steals our time and brings instant gratification.

TEMPTATION is giving into a desire because of a lie we are believing. We open the door to its power when we entertain wrong thoughts. While God always promises a way out, we still have to choose it. Sin and the result of it, whether it's ours or another's, has a destructive domino effect. When we give into temptation, it affects many.

BUSYNESS is the productivity trap. In the United States, we are the busiest we've ever been, and technology continues to propel us further into this black hole. We're so used to instant gratification we're losing the ability to trust and wait for God.

Do you make plans to read your bible and pray, only to run out of time? And when you do find the time, are you interrupted by a person, a situation or your own thoughts?

Do you ever read a passage in the Bible only to ask yourself what you've just read because your mind has wandered? Is this mere coincidence or spiritual resistance?

I struggle with depression and I'm often discontent with my own abilities. I tend to focus on my negatives. I'm distracted by what I think about myself, instead of what is true, or what God says about me. I don't see it as "worship," but that is exactly what I'm falling into—pride...self-worship...self-focus.

Sound familiar? We all have things that distract us. Whatever the enemy's tactic is for you, his goal is to keep you paralyzed from living out your calling just like he did with Eve. His deceitful ways are so indirect many times we don't even see him coming.

Lesson Learned:
Satan's harmful diversions need to be uncovered
and told where to go — back to hell where they belong!

The Noise Tactic

As Satan dropped his spiritually "dark crumbs" of doubt and confusion in front of Eve in Geneses 3:4–5, she took the bait. I can imagine an inner dialogue of noise that goes something like this to bring her to the point of no return:

Did God really say that or something else? Maybe Adam heard him wrong or misunderstood? Maybe it's not that bad. I mean it's so beautiful and looks delicious. It's the tree of knowledge. How could it be bad? Why wouldn't God want something like that for me? Is he holding me back from something great I could have? I want knowledge; I want to know both good and evil. Maybe he won't mind. Just one bite. I'll get Adam to eat it with me. What's the worst that could happen?

Eve allowed wrong thoughts and feelings a place in her mind. They multiplied, and Eve came under their spell. She chose to listen to the "noise" running rampant between her ears, instead of her Creator. Listening to runway thoughts led to her fateful choice of giving into desire and acting on a false belief. Noise can penetrate our minds in many ways, such as being alone and idle with our own thoughts, in self-induced cycles of busyness or through people and the circumstances of life.

Lesson Learned:
Learn from Eve: do not allow a noisy mind, nor let it persuade.
Halt runaway thoughts.

The woman was convinced. She saw that the tree was beautiful and its fruit looked delicious, and she wanted the wisdom it would give her. So she took some of the fruit and ate it. Then she gave some to her husband, who was with her, and he ate it, too (Genesis 3:6, NLT).

Eve was *convinced*, or in other words, believed Satan's lie. The Bible doesn't say anything about Eve being disingenuous in giving Adam the fruit. It does, however, say he was already with her and she gave it to him.

Was Adam aware of the snake's presence and his assault?
Could he hear or see him?

We don't exactly know the answers to these questions, nor do we know what Adam was doing at that moment. However, what we do know is that both Adam and Eve made their own choices, believed Satan's lies, and changed life forever.

What followed was a snowball effect.

At that moment their eyes were opened, and they suddenly felt shame at their nakedness. So they sewed fig leaves together to cover themselves... Then the LORD God called to the man, "Where are you?" He replied, "I heard you walking in the garden, so I hid. I was afraid because I was naked" (Genesis 3:7, 9-10, NLT).

The Accusation Tactic

SHAME. Adam and Eve felt its effects. God's original intent was for man to be unashamed, but unfortunately, with sin came humiliation and distress. Now, God intends for us to use these feelings for good.

While the accuser brings condemnation (life-stealing accusations which leads to oppression) when we sin, God brings conviction (an encouraging rebuke which leads to repentance). Satan loves to hurl his arrows of accusation. In fact, Revelation 12:10 says it's a constant action which will slowly wear us down if we are not combating them.

There are accusations of all sorts we can fall under. *I'm failing* is a nasty jab that tries to accuse me daily. Do you ever have negative thoughts that tear you down? Do you ever hear an inner dialogue saying *I'm a horrible person, I'm a hopeless case, or why would Jesus die for me?*

According to God's Word, these are all lies from the pit of hell. The Truth is, you were bought at a high price. In fact, it cost God His one and only Son. Sounds like you're pretty priceless to me!

Lesson Learned:
Receive conviction, not condemnation. Speak Romans 8:1,
"There is no condemnation for me because I belong to Christ Jesus."

The Isolation Tactic

SECLUSION. Adam and Eve *hid.* Do you ever want to be left alone or feel you are alone? Do you ever isolate yourself because you don't want others to know what you are doing or thinking? Do you ever want to hide from your problems and numb yourself with (alcohol, food, TV, sex, or place your "drug" of choice here) so you can get away from all the noise, accusations, worry and heaviness in your mind?

This state is where Adam and Eve found themselves, and unfortunately, we often follow their destructive example. Why do we try everything but running to the very One we are to *cast our cares on?* It's because we are being deceived!

Lesson Learned:
Isolation is Satan's plan, not God's.
Speak Ecclesiastes 4:12, "And though a man might prevail against one who is alone, two will withstand him—a threefold cord is not quickly broken."

The Fear Tactic

FEAR. Adam and Eve were *afraid*. They had messed up big time and were fearful of what that meant. Fear, just like worry, is an effective life stealer because it's constantly anticipating danger or some type of pain. Fear comes in many forms and is often hard to identify.

Up until a few years ago, I didn't see fear as my struggle. I was very wrong. Being overwhelmed and shutting down is a result of fear. Fear of failure and fear of rejection often try to suffocate me. Fear is a common and camouflaged part of the enemy's strategy.

Do you ever worry or obsess about letting others down? Or how about what others think? Are you constantly fighting for control? Do you worry about making mistakes even to the point of not doing anything at all? Or become consumed with the future or what hasn't happened yet? All of these scenarios involve worry. It's an indicator the fear tactic is being used.

Lesson Learned:
Speak 1 John 4:18, "Perfect love, casts out all fear..." and
Psalm 18:2, "The Lord is my rock and fortress..!"

The Blame Tactic

"Who told you that you were naked?" the LORD *God asked. "Have you eaten from the tree whose fruit I commanded you not to eat?" The man replied, "It was the woman you gave me who gave me the fruit, and I ate it." Then the* LORD *God asked the woman, "What have you done?" "The serpent deceived me," she replied. "That's why I ate it"* (Genesis 3:11-13, NLT).

BLAME. Adam blamed Eve (man); then Eve turned around and blamed the serpent (Satan).

This is the point in the story when you want to tsk, tsk, shake your head and basically blame them for this whole mess. Adam and Eve were guilty and neither one wanted to take responsibility for what they had done. I don't know about you, but I'm looking at myself in the mirror here. Hold on one second while I remove the plank out of my own eye!

We all do it. It's human instinct to want to blame anyone and anything but ourselves. It's the part of us that the serpent uses to tell us *we are not responsible* and leads us down a pathway of destruction. It is also what mocks the work of Christ. We cannot use man, what man has done or Satan as the scapegoat for our own actions. God gave each of us the gift of free will in action and what we choose to think on.

Lesson Learned:
We have a choice in every decision we make. Therefore, accept responsibility when you act AND Christ's covering of grace and forgiveness when you fail.

Consequences

With sin came consequence. Man and woman both experienced a spiritual death and separation from God. Eve's sin resulted in pain through childbirth and woman's desire to control her husband. Adam's sin resulted in the ground becoming cursed so man would labor at it all his life. These developments set the scene for a complex battlefield and equipped our enemy with multiple toxic arrows.

The good news? The story didn't end there. Our God is a just God. The serpent was not immune to consequence. God cursed him and made him grovel in the dust.

And God said to the serpent; "And I will put enmity between you and the woman, and between your offspring and hers; he will crush your head, and you will strike his heel" (Genesis 3:15, NLT).

There are three important points to see here:

1. The struggle is ongoing between Satan and man (Eve's offspring).
2. This event was no surprise to God. He is all-knowing and knew man would fail in his own strength.
3. The victory is ultimately ours through Christ.

Even before man was created, God knew and had a perfect plan in place. Jesus, our Savior, the offspring of Eve, would once and for all come to save man and crush the serpent's head.

Conclusion

We are in a battle with an enemy who has a specific plan to render our lives empty and useless. Since the time of Adam and Eve, the great deceiver has been studying mankind. And he is not alone. The book of Revelation speaks of an army of angels who fell to the earth with him. In Ephesians, Paul speaks of the powers and authorities as well as the devil, the commander of the unseen forces. If it's not him, it's a member of his army.

While there is no evidence the enemy can read our thoughts, he can read us through our reactions and choices. The enemy has seen what's happened in our childhood and in generations past, and what tendencies and weaknesses we have inherited. The enemy uses our circumstances to manipulate. He has learned our greatest fears, hang-ups, doubts, insecurities and sins. He's done his homework. We must do ours!

Satan and his army are crafty, but, God is greater!

BATTLE ORDERS
Ch 3 - The Thief's Plan

TAKEAWAYS: Identify three takeaways from this chapter. Share with a friend so they stick.

1.

2.

3.

REFLECTION: How might the enemy be using the following steal tactics in your life? Write out your answers in a separate journal, then discuss for clarity and accountability.

- Doubt
- Distraction
- Noise
- Accusation
- Isolation
- Fear
- Blame

BATTLE TOOL – Speak (Say Scripture)

The only power the enemy has over you is the deception you allow to remain. Locate one scripture you can use to avoid each of Satan's steal tactics above. Declare them out loud.

Ex: Distraction when trying to spend time with God.
Action: Speak Psalm 46:10, *"Be still and know that I am God."*

Ex: Fear when feeling overwhelmed or confused about a decision.
Action: Speak 2 Timothy 1:7, *"for God gave us a spirit not of fear but of power and love and self-control."*

*Go deeper verses from this chapter: 1 Corinthians 10:13; Deuteronomy 30:19; Psalm 55:22; Matthew 7:3.

4

THE ATTACK

But I am afraid that just as Eve was deceived by the serpent's cunning, your minds may somehow be led astray from your sincere and pure devotion to Christ.

— 2 CORINTHIANS 11:3, NIV

A TYPICAL DAY:

The sun rises and I wake to my clock blinking midnight. My plan for time with God is gone before my day begins. "I'm going to be so late! Why does this always happen?" I jump out of bed and rush through my morning routine.

I look in the mirror. Frizzy hair, wrinkles, extra pounds and stretch marks stare back at me. *God, I am so fat and ugly. Why did you make me this way?* I try on five different outfits before I find one that isn't too tight. Instant guilt and shame flood my mind thanks to the cookie dough I ate last night.

I wake the kids and meet resistance, defiance and fighting. *Why do they always do this? I bet it's my fault. My kids are messed up just like me.*

Amazingly, I find five minutes for God, but thoughts of my current financial situation invade. *We're never going to get out of this. How could we have been so stupid? I've got to figure out how to fix this...*

The front door shuts and I realize my husband left for work without saying goodbye. *Does he still love me? I wouldn't. I mean look at me. I bet he thinks this whole money thing is my fault. He is so selfish...*

The day's responsibilities bare down on my shoulders. Everything in me wants to shut down. I scroll through social media for a quick escape but instead find discouragement. *Why can't I have it all together like everybody else?*

I look at the pile of "to do's" on my desk, the clutter of my home and the meal schedule that doesn't reflect my reality. My older kids return from school and the mommy requests and needs increase. We sit down to a dinner of macaroni & cheese and frozen chicken nuggets, again.

All I want to do is hide. I head to my room for some silence, but instead, the mental torture only increases. *I'm failing. Nothing I do is ever good enough. No one appreciates me. I'm a lousy mom, wife, friend and overall person!*

When I finally get the kids to bed, there is nothing left for my husband. Fear washes over me as I begin to question. *Will we stay married after the kids leave? We are like roommates who don't even talk anymore.*

I enter into my nightly numbing ritual of mindless TV and sugary treats. Later my head hits the pillow with these final thoughts. *I hate my life. I've got to try harder tomorrow.*

For so long, I focused on what I could physically see and feel. Overtime this habit produced wrong thinking and an unhealthy mindset. There was no joy or peace. Past experiences, or my perception of them, created wrong beliefs over time about myself, others and my circumstances. What was happening today, or my perception of it, further confirmed these wrong beliefs and made them stronger. I was stuck in a destructive cycle doing the best I could while waiting for Jesus to take me away from the chaos.

The thief comes only to steal and kill and destroy. I came that they may have life and have it abundantly (John 10:10).

I was a Christian but living only one-third of John 10:10. I didn't understand Jesus gave His life not only to free me when I die, but also to give me a full, unique and abundant life now. I didn't recognize the spiritual resistance against me, nor did I remember that there was an even greater One for me. I didn't grasp the power and blessings already available to win the daily fight regardless of my circumstances. I was deceived. My mind was running rampant with lies, accusations, doubts and fear—flaming arrows from the evil one.

How do we get to these dark places of discontent and bitterness? The same ancient serpent who deceived Eve in the beginning is still using his same tactics, stealing from God's children however he can.

There are many believers living this way today. Are you one of them? The enemy is deviously working behind the scenes to steal from you. Look back at my example above and then think on your day. Look for any subtle assaults manifested through these three forms of attack.

The Attack of Circumstance

You keep him in perfect peace whose mind is stayed on you, because he trusts in you (Isaiah 26:3).

Job was a blameless and upright man who feared God and avoided evil. The Lord blessed him and he prospered in everything he did. That was until Satan came to God presenting an accusation. He claimed Job was protected from difficult circumstances. This was *why* Job was so "good," because he didn't have a reason not to be.

God allowed, not caused but allowed, the enemy to test Job

through circumstances. He set limitations, restraining Satan from physical harm to Job. Did Job pass the test? Yes, in the midst of difficulties and loss, Job chose to praise the Lord anyway.

Satan counterattacked with a second accusation, claiming Job remained faithful because God had not physically harmed him. Then, the Lord allowed Satan's attacks of infirmity, but once again set limitations to spare Job's life. Amidst tragedy, Job cried out in anguish, but still said nothing against God. The rest of the book of Job is spent in conversations with friends who came to Job's side with good intentions, but resulted in condemnation (Job 1–42 summarized).

While Satan cannot physically touch us, as we can see in Job's story, he has been known to attack through the manipulation of circumstances. At first glance, Job's story might seem a pointless tragedy, but a closer look reveals much:

- The enemy stands before God day and night with words of accusation against God's people.
- The enemy has to be granted permission to intervene. God is sovereign. He promises to never leave nor forsake us and nothing can happen without His allowance. This is a hard truth we can accept when we remember Romans 8:28, *And we know that for those who love God all things work together for good, for those who are called according to his purpose.*
- The enemy can have some say in the circumstances we face; however, the real battle is what we choose to do with the thoughts, feelings and perceptions we allow in those circumstances.

Circumstances are a minefield of their own. They distract and if we allow them to, will explode and rob us of our joy. Whether it's through the small and mundane like my example above or the extreme like Job's example, Satan is always looking for ways to wear us down and steal our peace.

I look at Job and recognize I cannot respond to life's circumstances in my own strength as he did. The good news is I don't have to. We have been given the Holy Spirit, God's Strength and Power, to overcome.

Lesson Learned:
Conquer the attack of any circumstance by remaining focused
on the Kingdom and empowered by the King.

The Attack of Other People

Make allowance for each other's faults and forgive anyone who offends you. Remember, the Lord forgave you, so you must forgive others (Colossians 3:13, NLT).

The enemy loves to manipulate and use the power of assumption to create counterfeit adversaries in our lives. These physical enemies can range from the obvious to the ever-so-subtle. Adolf Hitler, Osama Bin Laden and Charles Manson are just a few whose lives have represented all that is hateful.

The bad drivers, the ex-spouse, the annoying neighbor or the betraying friend are examples of familiar counterfeits who aren't necessarily evil; but they commit actions that steal our attention from God. Sure, there are times when we need to speak up and correct others, but most of the time it's about trusting God and His timing. Whomever it is for you, they are not the enemy; but instead, a diversion from the real culprit.

The Bible displays proof of this clever deception. Ezekiel 28 reveals references to Satan and the Fall. Its context, however, can be confusing, because the flesh and blood king of Tyre is also mentioned at the beginning of this funeral song.

Son of man, give the prince of Tyre this message from the Sovereign Lord: "In your great pride you claim, 'I am a god! I sit on a divine throne in the heart of the sea.' But you are only a man and not a god, though you boast that you are a god... I ordained and anointed you as the mighty angelic guardian. You had access to the holy mountain of God and walked among the stones of fire (Ezekiel 28:2,14, NLT).

We see the same thing in Isaiah 14, a taunt for the king of Babylon.

...you will taunt the king of Babylon. You will say, "The mighty man has been destroyed. Yes, your insolence is ended... How you are fallen from heaven, O shining star, son of the morning! You have been thrown down to the earth, you who destroyed the nations of the world (Isaiah 14:4, 12, NLT).

Both the kings of Tyre and Babylon are full of pride claiming they are God. In each instance, God is chastising the flesh and blood kings in His lament. However, a closer look reveals He is also talking to Satan, the spiritual mastermind behind the scenes.

While evil kings of the past and corrupt political figures of today are obvious scapegoats the enemy uses, Satan doesn't stop there. Sometimes, Satan craftily uses the good intentions of friends, like in Job's story, to discourage and distract.

Could it be the friends of Job and these evil kings are two extremes, but examples of the differing degrees of manipulation and deception the evil puppet master uses for his purposes?

In my life, I see times where both my family and friends have unknowingly been used against me. Conversely, I have also unintentionally hurt others. Satan can use even believer's well-meaning efforts to aid his plans.

Look closely at your life. Be aware and see through this deception. Your enemy is not people, it's Satan. He loves to cause disunity, especially among believers. Dissension between Christians most often comes down to misunderstandings, misconceptions and assumptions being fed to us by a third party. Reject Satan's plans to use people as his pawns in this spiritual chess match.

Lesson Learned:
Do not allow Satan to create counterfeit enemies
especially among other believers.

The Attack of the Mind

For the word of God is living and active, sharper than any two-edged sword, piercing to the division of soul and of spirit, of joints and of marrow, and discerning the thoughts and intentions of the heart (Hebrews 4:12).

Satan's steal tactics all originate in the mind—his most fruitful way to attack. Think about it: the attacks of circumstance and other people are only as powerful as our thoughts and attitudes about them.

Thoughts are constant. They run rampant between our ears. In fact, *Discover Magazine*, through various research studies, determined we have somewhere between 20,000 to 600,000 thoughts per day. While this is a wide spectrum, we can be sure of one thing, We are doing a whole lot of thinking.

We aren't aware of most of our thoughts. Did you know our brains have to think to breathe? Plus, there are a vast number of thoughts in our subconscious that we repeat over and over. While some are based on biological instinct, many are shaped by our past, present and the way we view our future.

Other interesting studies have revealed 98 percent of today's thoughts are the same as yesterday's and 80 percent are negative (*Change Your Mind, Change Your Brain* by Sharon Begley). That's pretty scary. So how many of our thoughts are actually true?

Negative messages build up over time and increase in potency as we think and focus on them. Most often, the negative messages we receive from a situation are either false or partial information. In addition, since other individuals are usually involved, their thoughts and feelings further complicate the situation. Our minds are not just playing tricks on us. This is spiritual and we're being held captive by our thinking!

Lesson Learned:
Set your hope on God's Word instead of our limited thinking.

The Human Condition

Understanding the mind's role in this battle is key. We cannot direct our energy toward hurtful people, tragic events or unfortunate circumstances because they are merely decoys. No matter what our day holds – whether tough circumstance, close proximity to a counterfeit enemy or just the mundane – we are always thinking and processing through the "life lenses" we choose.

A mind set on what's seen only sees a partial reality and responds accordingly. Our perspective of past experiences shapes our perspectives today, creating further harm. Satan uses this to his advantage. Take marriage for example. Spouses normally come from different backgrounds and experiences making marriage relationships complex.

When my husband left for work without saying goodbye, my first thought was that he was mad and punishing me. This simple act forced my insecurities and fear of rejection into overdrive. I then compared our relationship to the Hallmark movie I'd just seen on TV and began to doubt my husband's love for me.

My husband had no idea I was feeling this way. He was distracted with work and simply forgot to say goodbye. He didn't realize this was such a big deal because his family of origin communicates and connects differently from mine.

Here are a few other examples to help spark personal revelation:

- A person who grew up without a father figure can struggle with thoughts of rejection as well as misperceptions about their Heavenly Father. Situations occurring today can trigger a need to control relationships or sudden outbursts of anger.
- A person who was raised in a critical or legalistic environment can struggle with thoughts of inadequacy and insecurity as an adult. Perfectionism or isolation (fight or flight) can become coping mechanisms.
- Someone who experienced abuse in their early years may struggle with low self-worth and addictions. They may also struggle with intimacy and keep people at a distance for protection.

This is the human condition. After a hard day, instinct is to focus on what we see and feel. We then shut down in disappointment by finding comfort in a "drug" of choice instead of resting in The Comforter. Life throws us so many scenarios and there are many factors involved. Spiritual lenses and introspection are needed for all of us to correctly assess what is true.

Enslaved Thinking

It is for freedom that Christ has set us free. Stand firm, then, and do not let yourselves be burdened again by a yoke of slavery (Galatians 5:1, NIV).

After decades of pastoring and counseling, Dr. Neil Anderson of Freedom in Christ Ministries came up with an astounding statistic. He concluded that no more than 15 percent of evangelical Christians are completely free of Satan's bondage. Bondage means the state of being a slave, or the opposite of free. Is this statistic true?

According to Galatians 5:1, all Christ followers have been set free.

Past tense. That means freedom has already been given to all believers, not just 15 percent of them. This verse also warns believers to not fall back into a yoke, or burden, of slavery. Our enemy is good at deceiving people into believing they are still slaves or in bondage to something. If Dr. Anderson's findings are true, then a large majority (approximately 8 out of 10 Christ followers) are free, but don't feel or believe it. This is a serious problem.

If the majority of Satan's attacks are in the mind, then 85 percent of Christ followers are allowing themselves to be in bondage, believing a huge lie.

Lesson Learned:
If we believe we are enslaved, then we will live like we are. If we believe the Truth – that we are free through Christ – then we will live free.

Where We Focus Makes a Difference

The enemy works tirelessly to fill our minds with lies. He uses others and our circumstances to do it. He knows if we take hold of a lie, he gains the ground needed to steal, kill and destroy the roots of God's Word embedded in our hearts. This is Truth but not where we are to focus.

Take caution not to fall into one of the following categories:

- *A believer who focuses too much on Satan and his method of attack.* This person seems to forget *Who* is really fighting for them and that God is already victorious. They speak and think about their enemy all the time, often giving him too much credit. Although the father of lies can persuade us, our actions are still our choice and we must take responsibility for them. This person is driven by fear or striving to overcome the enemy in their own strength.

- *A believer who focuses on what they can see and dismisses the power of Satan.* This person thinks their enemy is who or what they are fighting in the moment. They are oblivious to the real battle as they set their eyes on counterfeits. This group spends their time fighting physically and getting nowhere. They miss the spiritual component present and, therefore, the power of God that they can access as a believer.

A healthy awareness of our enemy is what's necessary if we are to be victorious in this battle. To walk a healthy balance, we need to be conscious of the thief, but not focused on him.

Jesus is the only One worthy of our focus. He promises the key to peace and freedom is through setting our minds on Him, remaining in Him, and submitting to Him. That is exactly where I want to be. How about you? If we are focused on Satan, our mind is not set on God.

Lesson Learned:
Be aware of the thief, but not afraid of or focused on him.

Conclusion

Knowing God's Word gives us the power to see clearly, recognize attacks and overcome enslaved thinking. In order for Truth to set us free, we must believe it. Truth must root itself in the heart. Let's do our part and trust God to do His.

- Pray and speak scripture.
- Listen for and identify wrong thoughts and mental messages.
- Ask for wisdom and strength to shut down wrong thinking before it's internalized.

Seeing what's true about ourselves, other people, and our circumstances is needed for battle.

BATTLE ORDERS
Ch 4 – The Attack

TAKEAWAYS:

1.

2.

3.

REFLECTION: Wrestle with the following questions. Write out your answers in a separate journal, then discuss for clarity and accountability.

1. In what ways can you identify with my example at the beginning of the chapter (i.e. thoughts, feelings, circumstances)?
2. How have you fallen prey to fighting the strategy (circumstances, other people or your thoughts and feelings) instead of the strategist?
3. In what ways have you fallen into enslaved thinking?

BATTLE TOOL: Write (Take Mental Inventory)

What occurs during your day? From the circumstances (big and small) that you face, the thoughts and feelings you experience, and the words and/or actions that follow.

1. Write down in your journal anything that comes to mind
2. Review your findings and ask yourself "why" (*e.g., why did I feel this way? Why did I do that?*). Write down anything else that comes to mind.
3. Identify the thief's steal, kill and destroy plan in your life.
4. Don't allow discouragement! This process takes time and starts with forming a habit of identifying what you are thinking and feeling.

*Go deeper verses from this chapter: Revelation 12:10; Isaiah 26:3; John 8:31-32; James 4:7.

5

GOD'S PLAN

...I came that they may have and enjoy life, and have it in abundance *[to the full, till it overflows].*

— JOHN 10:10B, AMP

MONROE, LOUISIANA 2015

We headed west to visit a good friend from college. My kids were so excited they had a pool in their backyard, so this was where we spent most of our time. My youngest, Allie, could not yet swim, so I made sure she was always wearing her safety float. It only came off when we went inside to use the restroom.

While I was waiting for my daughter to finish in the restroom, I started talking with my girlfriend and didn't notice Allie slip out the back door unprotected.

Here's a circumstance that could have turned tragic. *Was this an attack from the enemy? Maybe.*

All of a sudden, I got a sick feeling in my gut then proceeded to look for Allie. *Was this the Holy Spirit nudging me? Probably.*

I ran outside and found her in the middle of the pool under water. I jumped in and immediately pulled her into my arms. Thankfully she was safe.

I tell you this story to share an example of Satan's assaults we can have power over. Yes, we can do our part to avoid certain circumstances, but, like this example, some just happen. While we can't control events, we can control our responses to them. Satan's attack that day was not the circumstance of Allie getting in the pool unprotected. The attack was the spiritual jabs that started flooding my mind afterward.

- I could have let the tactics of fear and accusation take hold and consume my thoughts. *Shame on me. I'm a horrible mom. How could I let that happen? What if she had died? I can't ever let her out of my sight again.*
- I could've fallen into blame and isolation. *I hate myself. How could I be so careless? Why haven't I gotten her swimming lessons? My friend's house is not safe. She distracted me. We have to leave.*
- I could have started doubting God and His love. *God, how can you let things like this happen? I can't trust You with my children.*

Thankfully, because I recognized the attacks or thoughts invading my mind, I chose to speak against them. "God, thank you for protecting my daughter. You love us and have good plans. I trust You in all things and with all things. I will not fear, for You will never leave or forsake me."

Now, I know all circumstances don't have as good of an ending. However, Job has shown us that even in the most tragic of circumstances, we can still overcome the enemy's attacks. It is only possible through the Holy Spirit where we receive the power to walk through any circumstance.

I have to remind myself often of God's sovereignty. He is never at any moment surprised by the battle, or circumstances, we find ourselves in. Never. And He can always bring beauty for ashes. Always. Therefore, we can trust our Commanding Officer and His perfect plan.

God's Unchanging Blueprint

From the beginning, God has always been in control and working out His perfect plan. Out of love, He created man and gave him the ability to choose. Unfortunately, when tested, man chose to disobey. This resulted in spiritual blindness. As sin entered the world, mankind lost his right standing and direct connection to God.

In the first five books of the Bible, God laid out the law through Moses. Throughout the Old Testament, mankind shows its inability to live up to the law and make the continual blood sacrifices required in exchange for restoration and forgiveness. Many prophets would come, calling man to return to God and obey, but God's creation would continually fall prey to the pull of sin. Again, this was no surprise.

God the Son was there from the beginning, waiting patiently for His role in the story to unfold and the perfect moment to enter the scene. He came to earth to defeat death on the cross, becoming our permanent blood sacrifice. Because of Jesus Christ, a supernatural reversal occurred. Believers received Christ's righteousness instead of their own. Jesus took the penalty for sin so the blood sacrifice and requirement of the law could be made perfect and complete for all who believe.

God's plan all along was for Jesus to bridge the way back to the Father. Christ's work on the cross granted full reconciliation to all of God's children. Not a barely making it life until He comes back to get us, but an abundant, rich and satisfying life right now!

Abundance is Now

The life Christ died to give us doesn't start when we die. It started at salvation, when we received His life over our own. The tragedy is many believers are blinded to this Truth, because their thoughts tell them otherwise.

For example, if I asked you what life is about, what would you say? Unfortunately, many believers would say it's about just pushing through or surviving until Christ returns, and as we wait, trying to save as many people as we can. This was me for many years as the enemy continued to steal all he could. Now, if you asked an unbeliever the same question, many would say life's about enjoying today and making the best of what we're given.

Could it be unbelievers are onto something we have missed? John 10:10 says Jesus came to set us free and give believers a rich and satisfying life. This richness, however, isn't in regards to a physical abundance such as material items or even an easy life; but instead, something much greater, spiritual abundance.

> If we are the ones who've been given the fullness of Christ, shouldn't we be the ones truly living?

Unfortunately, this is not the case as we look around or even in the mirror and see expressions of fatigue, discouragement, hopelessness and entrapment. If believers are God's walking advertisements to a dying world and this was what they see, why would unbelievers want what we have?

No wonder there are so many lost souls and believers who are barely making it. We have been deceived. Our eyes have been blinded to Ephesians 1:18-19 (NIV):

- The hope to which God has called us to.
- The riches of His glorious inheritance.
- The incomparably great power within for us who believe.

Hope. Riches. Power. These divine gifts are already ours. Do you believe this? Have you received this? If your honest answer is "no", then there is a wrong thought(s) keeping you from this Truth. Our deceiver loves to plant the lie that *abundance is something you have to work towards or cannot obtain.*

Ephesians 2:8-9 contradicts that lie. *For by grace you have been saved through faith. And this is not your own doing; it is the gift of God, not a result of works, so that no one may boast.*

God makes no mistakes. His intricate plan of grace always overrides the thief's plan. God is inviting us to *see* what's true and *fight* the battle for what's already ours. If we will choose to grant Jesus full access of ourselves (including our thoughts), then spiritual abundance will multiply and heavenly treasures will abound.

A Typical Day – Take Two:

The sun rises and I wake to my clock blinking midnight. I overslept, so I jump out of bed, rush through my morning routine and begin my dialogue with God. "Heavenly Father, this is the day you have made; I will rejoice and be glad in it. I invite you into my whole day. Please show me what it is to look like. Give me the power and desire to do what pleases you."

I look in the mirror and choose Truth instead of my feelings and what my brokenness sees. "I praise you for I am fearfully and wonderfully made. My body is your temple and I will not tear down your creation with negative talk."

I wake the kids and meet resistance, defiance and fighting. "Thank you for these little blessings you have entrusted to me. Give me patience and wisdom as we train them up in the way they should go. Help me to trust you and enjoy this season of life."

Amazingly, I find five minutes to sit with God, but thoughts of my current financial situation invade. "God, thank you for your constant presence. I give you this burden and will not be anxious. You are so much bigger and you supply all of my needs according to your riches!"

The front door shuts and I realize my husband left for work without saying goodbye. "Father, my feelings are trying to get the best of me right now. I choose to be thankful for my husband instead. Help me to love him the way You love me."

The day's responsibilities bear down on my shoulders. Everything in me wants to shut down. I scroll through social media for a quick escape but instead find discouragement. "I will not compare myself or my life to others. Remind me God that You are my audience of one. Help me not to conform to the ways of the world."

I look at the pile of "to do's" on my desk, the clutter of my home, and my meal schedule that doesn't reflect reality. My older kids return from school and the mommy requests and needs increase. I take a deep breath and sit my family down to a dinner of macaroni & cheese and frozen chicken nuggets. "Thank you, Lord, for your provisions."

When I want to hide, I take a moment, get on my knees, and start praying. "Jesus, help me to be more like you. I choose to live in your abundance. I am free and I receive your grace. There is no condemnation for me because I am in Christ. Jesus, thank you for giving me your righteousness!"

When I finally get the kids to bed, I'm exhausted. "Father, I trust you in this season. I receive your strength as I surrender my marriage to you."

Instead of my nightly numbing ritual, I choose to seek rest and comfort in my Sustainer. "God, thank you for carrying my burdens and giving me your peace and comfort today. You are all I need after a hard day. Thank you that I don't have to do this alone and that you are always in control. I receive your mercies for they are new each day!"

(Refer back to the beginning of Chapter 4
to compare the different responses.)

From Enslaved to Abundance

Can your day look exactly the same on the outside, yet tremendously different on the inside? The answer is yes, when you choose a different perspective. The enemy used to steal my abundance, even in the mundane. Not anymore. What changed? My circumstances definitely did not; but my thinking did. I began implementing *The Believer's Battle Strategy.*

- Seeing the enemy's approach and God's victorious plan over it.
- Seeing beyond the physical and trusting the spiritual.
- Choosing to base my joy on the Lord, instead of what was going on or what people were doing.
- Seeking His peace in the midst of chaos.
- Choosing to believe His promises over my feelings.

Now, I know there are some who either want to punch me in the face right now, or walk away from this book because *this kind of change is impossible in your situation.* If this is you, recognize the assault and claim the following:

For God is working in you, giving you the <u>desire</u> and the <u>power</u> to do what pleases him (Philippians 2:13, NLT, emphasis mine).

I can do all things through him (Christ) who strengthens me (Philippians 4:13).

This change in perspective is not easy. In fact, it's brutal, especially at first. There are still times I have to force myself to act and times I still fail; however, daily progress is being made. I can choose to speak right and act right even when I don't feel like it. If I do this consistently, my thoughts will eventually follow. God promises His Words are not empty. They have life-changing power!

Each day, I have an opportunity to re-train my brain and live in abundance instead of remaining enslaved. This attitude shift was life-altering for me, and it can be for you too. The more we practice a new habit, the easier it becomes. This is faith: believing even when we do not yet *see* or feel. Transformation comes by combating the thief's plan and instead choosing to live out God's plan.

Lesson Learned:
To activate your faith and increase your abundance, speak and think on God's promises even when you can't yet see it or feel it.

Abundance is Fruit

The thief's plan is to *steal* our abundance or the Light inside, but God's plan is for us to fully experience Christ. While Satan cannot take the light of Jesus away from us, he can dim our glow and experience so we cannot see God's Truth clearly. This glow is the great gift of the Holy Spirit deposited into each of us at salvation. He pours out His powerful presence onto believers and flows through them in the form of fruit, spiritual fruit.

> *But the Holy Spirit produces this kind of fruit in our lives: love, joy, peace, patience, kindness, goodness, faithfulness, gentleness, and self-control* (Galatians 5:22-23a, NLT).

How can we know when the enemy is attacking? By looking at our spiritual fruit. An attack is when we feel our Spirit-given fruit like peace, joy or patience being stolen. It's when we are tempted and self-control is needed, but we don't feel strong enough. It's when we experience doubt, double-mindedness or unbelief. It's when we get angry and don't want to show love, kindness, goodness or gentleness to our offender.

All of these are indicators an attack is occurring. And the majority of the time, the attack originates from a perceived thought about a situation – not reality. Do not let the thief steal your fruit!

I'm determined to keep my peace and joy. Regardless of what I see or feel, I have to speak God's Word and sing His praises instead of dwelling on what's hurtful, frustrating or inconvenient. Doing so sends the enemy an important message: *Stop messing with me because I'm a child of God and I see what you are doing!*

Lesson learned:
We send the enemy messages by how we respond to our situations.

Abundance is Spiritual

The thief's plan is to *destroy* our abundance by twisting the concept, but God's plan is for us to experience true abundance. The world sees abundance as the acquiring of more and more (i.e. wealth, material items and power) *through effort.* In addition, believers have even been deceived into thinking abundance is an easy life. We think if we're not experiencing ease, then we're doing something wrong.

The abundance Jesus speaks of in John 10:10, real abundance, is living in the free offering of Christ's fullness in your circumstances *through grace alone.*

God reveals true abundance through some main Bible characters.

KING SOLOMON of the Old Testament, who *surpassed all the kings of the earth in riches and wisdom,* quickly learned earthly abundance was merely a counterfeit to the real thing. In fact, it was a trap. King Solomon passionately pleaded for us to learn from his mistake.

So I came to hate life because everything done here under the sun is so troubling. Everything is meaningless – like chasing the wind (Ecclesiastes 2:17, NLT).

In the world's eyes, Solomon had everything. Yet, he was empty. He learned the hard way that fame, intellect, power, pleasure and money are not what fills. We see this same story playing out today with many of the wealthy, corporately successful and famous still searching through acquiring more, only to end in divorce, addiction, bankruptcy, loneliness and even suicide.

THE APOSTLE PAUL, on the other hand, regularly suffered and was homeless the majority of his ministry. In fact, he had nothing in the world's eyes, but spiritually speaking, he had everything that mattered. He learned *the secret of being content whatever the situation* was through Christ, and passionately pleaded Philippians 1:21, *to live is Christ, and to die is gain.*

JESUS THE MESSIAH lived a life without wealth, popularity, or worldly pleasures. In fact, he came from very humble beginnings and was put to death like a violent criminal. Yet, He is true abundance.

Lesson Learned:
True abundance is not of this world.
It is peace amidst circumstance, joy amidst mourning, and trusting God's ways even when they don't make sense or provide comfort or wealth.

Abundance is Christ

The thief's plan was to *kill* our abundance, but God's sovereign plan prevailed! I'm sure the thief thought he had it all figured out that fateful day when Jesus, who is Abundance, hung on the cross and breathed his last breath. Satan's plan backfired three days later when Jesus once and for all defeated death and its power over His people.

God the Son, our crucified and resurrected Savior, now sits at the right hand of God the Father. He was spoken of in the Word way before He came to earth. In the Old Testament, the prophet Isaiah foretold of the Messiah to come and this new life He offered.

Come, everyone who thirsts, come to the waters; and he who has no money, come, buy and eat! Come, buy wine and milk without money and without price. Why do you spend your money for that which is not bread, and your labor for that which does not satisfy? Listen diligently to me, and eat what is good, and delight yourselves in rich food (Isaiah 55:1-2).

COME AND DRINK! IT'S FREE! When I read this Old Testament verse, John 4 of the New Testament comes to mind. Jesus is resting at a well when an outcast woman comes to collect water. He recognizes the woman's true need and offers her the cure, Himself.

Jesus said to her, "Everyone who drinks of this water will be thirsty again, but whoever drinks of the water that I will give him will never be thirsty again. The water that I will give him will become in him a spring of water welling up to eternal life" (John 4:13-14).

We are all looking for something that fills. We seek nourishment from the things of this world only to remain empty wanting more and believing the lie that *"it" will eventually satisfy*. This is Satan using our flesh and the world's ways against us. Earthly things will never bring what we're looking for. True satisfaction and nourishment is only found in Jesus.

Lesson Learned:
Abundance is Jesus and offered to all who are thirsty.

Abundance is Knowing the Word

In the beginning was the Word, and the Word was with God, and the Word was God (John 1:1).

The flesh screams for desserts and candy, but healthy nourishment is what our physical bodies really need in order to thrive. Just like our bodies need to remain correctly fueled, so do our spirits. Our spiritual nourishment is Jesus, both the Living Water and the Word. Someone who is empty or isn't getting their "daily nourishment" will suffer from a spiritual deficiency and thus miss out on their true abundance.

Revisiting Isaiah reveals three instructions
on how to avoid spiritual deficiency.

Incline your ear, and come to me; hear, that your soul may live; and I will make with you an everlasting covenant, my steadfast, sure love for David... For my thoughts are not your thoughts, neither are your ways my ways, declares the Lord..."For as the rain and the snow come down from heaven and do not return there but water the earth, making it bring forth and sprout, giving seed to the sower and bread to the eater, so shall my word be that goes out from my mouth (Isaiah 55:3, 8, 10-11a);

1. *Listen* to God alone – not Satan, the world or your sinful desires.
2. *Focus* on God and His Truth – not the world's counterfeit.´
3. *Trust* God even when we don't understand.

LISTEN. FOCUS. TRUST. These are all "present tense" words of action. Together, let's intentionally create space *today* and clear our minds of noise *today* so we can see and hear Truth instead of lies *today*.

So shall my word be that goes out from my mouth; it shall not return to me empty, but it shall accomplish that which I purpose, and shall succeed in the thing for which I sent it (Isaiah 55:11-12).

God's Word was sent to open our eyes and set us free. The Word became flesh and we have seen His glory. The Word of God is our all-sustaining and fully satisfying nourishment. It is our weapon and the key to abundant thinking.

Lesson Learned:
God's Word always speaks and will not return void.

Conclusion

Believers, we are called to abundance, a plentiful and overly sufficient life. Stop and read that again. When you walk in Christ and fully embrace what God says, you aren't just enough, you are *more* than enough! To step out into your God-given abundance and participate in His perfect plan:

- Stay Alert
- Remain God Focused
- Exercise Word power

For you shall go out in joy and be led forth in peace; (Isaiah 55:12a).

This is abundant thinking.

BATTLE ORDERS
Ch 5 - God's Plan

TAKE AWAYS

1.

2.

3.

REFLECTION: Wrestle with the following questions. Write out your answers in a separate journal, then discuss for clarity and accountability.

1. Finish this statement with what you believe: "Abundance is…."
2. What scripture verse(s) back up your belief? If your answer does not line up with Truth, correct it by seeking the Truth in scripture.
3. How are you living now in the abundance God speaks of? If you are not, what step can you take today towards abundant thinking?

BATTLE TOOL: Combat (Truth Binder)

Allow God's Word to become your ammunition. Select a notecard system (whether a flash card app on your phone or a flip notecard binder. I personally prefer the latter) to keep God's written Word (scripture) ready and easily accessible.

1. Locate scriptures from the Bible that speak to you and refute lies you have come to believe.
2. Record these verses in the system you chose – this is your Truth Binder.
3. Read, meditate, declare and speak your verses aloud against the enemy's lies!
4. Keep your Truth Binder on hand and use it to combat wrong thinking and negative feelings.
5. Speak the Word when you:

- feel yourself losing peace, joy, or patience.
- experience any negative feelings.
- are angry about something that just happened.
- feel condemnation for something you have just done, etc.

If you don't have a specific verse to claim over your situation, speak aloud the mighty name of Jesus!

*Go deeper verses from this chapter: Psalm 22:6, 118:25, 139:14; Philippians 2:13, 4:11-13,19; 1 Corinthians 6:19; Psalm 22:6; Romans 8:1, 12:2; Matthew 11:28-30; Lamentations 3:22-23; 1 Kings 10:23; John 1:14.

6

GOD'S POWER

He will cover you with his feathers. He will shelter you with his wings. His faithful promises are your armor and protection.

— PSALM 91:4, NLT

SUMMER 2012

I had a miscarriage early in pregnancy. I remember the moment I realized what was happening. I felt my mind returning to a dark miry pit and my heart shutting down in pain. I recognized this unfortunate circumstance was happening, but more so that Satan was trying to take advantage of this opportunity. He jumped on the chance to flood my mind with discouragement, sadness and anger towards God.

In that moment, I remembered a visual from a Joyce Meyer's TV teaching on the Armor of God. She lifted up a knight's shield to deflect the enemy's arrows. As she performed this action, she spoke out in faith, "I trust you God. You've got this." As I watched this visual play out in my head, I chose to perform the same action. I lifted my unseen "shield" and in faith spoke aloud those same words.

Immediately, I felt Satan's arrows lose their power. A protection of light and comfort came over my mind and heart. Of course, this was a circumstance where I needed to allow myself to grieve, but I could now do it in the arms of my Comforter. As I walked through the grieving process that day, I took my two boys to the beach and chose a posture of thankfulness in the midst of this tough circumstance. There were plenty of moments where those darts returned at full force, but I continued lifting my faith shield and speaking of my good God whom I can trust in all things!

God desires for us to experience His presence and power. Psalm 91:4 (NLT) says *He will cover you with his feathers. He will shelter you with his wings. His faithful promises are your armor and protection.* As I read this, I envision God as a vast and immovable strength standing right behind me. His face is just beyond my grasp to see, but His welcoming arms reveal a wingspan covering of love and protection. What do you see?

Through the divine sacrificial blood of Jesus Christ, all of God's children are covered and sheltered in this life as well as the one to come. While I am ready for the next life to come, I must not miss the fullness of God's plans for me in this life. Believers, we've been given the opportunity to powerfully participate in spiritual battle right now.

Psalm 91 goes on to say if we make the Lord our refuge and shelter, no evil will conquer. We can be spiritually exempt from harm right now because we are divinely protected. However, there is a prerequisite to receiving this power. We have to put it on.

Put Your "Power" on

I have this task that has to be done. This place I need to go. But no matter how hard I try, I just can't seem to get there. Attempt after attempt leaves me right where I started. I look around and see people everywhere doing what they are supposed to. *Why can't I? Why do I feel so … vulnerable? What am I missing?*

I look down and then it hits me. I'm exposed. Yep, no clothes. How did I forget my clothes? The harder I try to find something to cover up with, the more exposed I become. Frustration and anxiety wash over me and park themselves to stay as I continue in a labyrinth with no covering or way out.

Am I the only one who has had these bizarre dreams? I will go somewhere important only to find myself wearing a bathing suit or heaven forbid, nothing at all. When my nights are spent caught up in these odd scenarios, I wake up emotionally spent. Anxiousness and frustration often follow me throughout my day.

Spiritually, this is a picture of what many of us do every day. We walk out into the world completely exposed to the enemy and his assaults. No wonder stress and worry cling to us like a parasite. How often do we walk through life spiritually unprotected? How can we expect to win our daily battles if we are unarmed and exposed?

It is only through walking in God's power that we overcome the daily schemes of Satan. Unfortunate circumstances and complex relationships are unavoidable; however, we're granted God's constant power and protection in the midst of them. Abba Father has stretched out His everlasting arms to shelter His children, and His wings are impenetrable.

> Not only have we been given *protective* power,
> we've also been given fierce *proactive* power.

Psalm 91:13 says we will trample upon lions and serpents and they will be crushed. If we make the Lord our refuge and remain firmly grounded in His promises, we are unstoppable! Seems impossible, but with God all things are possible and He has chosen each of us for such a time as this.

The Armor of God

Soldiers do not walk into battle without their protective clothing and necessary artillery. They are trained to expect the unexpected. If they are not properly covered at all times, they become an easy target. Furthermore, if they do not utilize the resources they've been trained to fight with, battle wounds are inevitable and defeat is likely.

Believers, as soldiers in spiritual battle the same holds true for us. The Armor of God is God's power and protection to be worn and utilized every day. Putting on God's Armor is:

OUR PROTECTIVE COATING. It is not a heavy or bulky burden like we imagine a knight's armor in medieval times. On the contrary, God's "burden" is light, and His yoke is easy.

Put on all of God's armor so that you will be able to stand firm against all strategies of the devil (Ephesians 6:11, NLT).

A DAILY AND NECESSARY RITUAL. Every day that we clothe ourselves with God's power, we transfer our worldly perspective to a Kingdom one. When we can see clearly, we can fight victoriously.

For we are not fighting against flesh-and-blood enemies, but against evil rulers and authorities of the unseen world, against mighty powers in this dark world, and against evil spirits in the heavenly places (Ephesians 6:12, NLT).

A PROCESS. I cannot expect my clothes to magically appear on my body when I step into my closet. Nor can I expect to be completely dressed and ready in one simple action. Our morning routines involve many steps, each serving a specific purpose. God's Armor is the same. While we are freely given our full armor, in order for it to be utilized correctly, each piece must be worn.

Therefore, put on every piece of God's armor so you will be able to resist the enemy in the time of evil. Then after the battle you will still be standing firm (Ephesians 6:13, NLT).

Developing a daily plan to get "spiritually dressed" is key to achieving victory in combat. God's Armor is our undefeatable resource we are to train in. Just knowing about your armor will not bring victory, but actively wearing and exercising it daily will.

Belt of Truth

So stand firm and hold your ground, having tightened the wide band of truth (personal integrity, moral courage) around your waist (Ephesians 6:14a, AMP).

TRUTH. It is the Word of God, the voice of God and the Holy Spirit's discernment in our relationships and circumstances. To know Truth, we must feed on Truth, fix our minds and hearts on Truth, surround ourselves with Truth or in other words, wear it like a belt holding us securely.

My daddy always wore a belt, whether dressed up for work or laboring in the yard. I didn't wear belts until after I had children and my body changed. Certain areas went flat and I found myself having to wear my belt just so I wouldn't sport the plumber look and scar innocent bystanders. I'd start my day with everything in place – my jeans fitted and crisp – and then somewhere along the way, I'd find myself constantly pulling them back up to stay in place. If I didn't eventually put on a belt, my pants would fall off.

Just like those jeans, we put on Truth and are ready for our day. As the day wears on, we get worn and have to constantly pull ourselves back up. If we aren't filling our minds back up with Truth, we will become exposed.

Ephesians 6:14 states we're not only to wear our Truth belt, but to actively "tighten" it. Tightening, or strengthening, Truth in our lives comes through reading, studying, speaking aloud and listening to God's Word. Truth doesn't only come through reading the Word, but please hear me, it never contradicts it. The Spirit often speaks in our circumstances. He will also bring *Truth tellers* into our life. Watch for them and surround yourself with them instead of the story tellers, or friends who tell you what you want to hear.

To follow Christ is to allow God to transform you to be more like Christ. As you grow closer to Him and continually tighten your Truth, you decrease as He increases. This Truth tightening process is continuous for we will never know all there is this side of heaven.

God never stops speaking through His Word; therefore, never stop tightening your Truth. Otherwise humility will diminish and pride will set in. Pride is the enemy's playground.

Lesson Learned:
God is always speaking. Humbly look and listen
for Him to reveal His Truth daily.

Breastplate of Righteousness

... and having put on the breastplate of righteousness (an upright heart),
(Ephesians 6:14b, AMP).

RIGHTEOUSNESS. It is blamelessness. Satan, who is the complete opposite, likes to feed us lies that *we need to work for our own righteousness* or that *we aren't worthy of it*. This takes our focus off of God and places it onto ourselves or the world where we strive to prove our worth.

Our breastplate is vital because it protects our heart, and who we truly are. This is what the enemy is after and where the majority of deception lies. He comes at our heart through the mind by telling us how unworthy and wrong we are. Forgetting who and Whose we are is a constant life-stealing trap many fall into. If our heart is not being protected, we will lose the daily battle.

The breastplate is also unique because it's the one piece of armor we cannot put on ourselves. Why? Because Romans 3:10 says that none are righteous. Christ is the only righteous One and He died to give His righteousness to us. We cannot put His righteousness on, because it's not ours. We receive the Breastplate of Righteousness by allowing the Holy Spirit, our constant Armor Bearer and deposit guarantee of Christ in us, to put it in place as we humbly recognize there is nothing we can do to earn it.

Attaining righteousness was never our burden to carry, but there are times I will start my day with my breastplate on and old thinking patterns will resurface. When I allow this, I pick my works burden back up, believe the world instead of the Word and my breastplate shifts out of place. Each time this happens, I must seek out my Armor Bearer immediately so He can re-adjust it.

Lesson Learned:
It is not my righteousness I'm receiving; therefore,
there is nothing Satan can tell me about what I've done
or been through to keep me from being made right.

Shoes of Peace

... and having strapped on your feet the gospel of peace in preparation [to face the enemy with firm-footed stability and the readiness produced by the good news] (Ephesians 6:15, AMP).

PEACE. It is freedom from strife. God spoke the World into being and holds all things in His hands. Out of all creation, who does God care about the most? It's us, His children, whom He delights in and breathed life into. Therefore, as Matthew 6:33-34 (NLT) states, *Seek the Kingdom of God above all else, live righteously, don't worry about tomorrow and he will give you everything you need.*

Truth brings peace. Peace comes through looking spiritually and seeing the following:

- Nothing will happen without God's allowance (Lamentations 3:37).
- Life will not end a moment sooner than God has planned (Job 14:5).
- Life is short, eternity is forever (2 Corinthians 4:16-18).
- This is not our home (Philippians 3:20).
- God cares about even the mundane of our lives (Luke 12:6-7).
- God will never abandon, leave or reject us (Deuteronomy 31:8).

God wants us to live life knowing that no matter what's going on, "He's got this." In John 14:27 (NIV), Jesus says *Peace I leave with you; my peace I give you. I do not give to you as the world gives. Do not let your hearts be troubled and do not be afraid.* That means we not only have peace, we have God's peace!

Picture it: You sliding your feet into fuzzy slippers. These are your Shoes of Peace. They make you feel warm, comfortable, and safe.

Knowing God's peace reveals counsel and comfort and is only possible through the Holy Spirit. If we grant Him full access to our entire day no matter what it brings, He will grant us wisdom and comfort in the midst of it.

Lesson Learned:
Keep your mind set on God no matter what the day holds,
and you will experience His perfect peace (Isaiah 26:3).

Shield of Faith

Above all, lift up the [protective] shield of faith with which you can extinguish
all the flaming arrows of the evil one (Ephesians 6:16, AMP).

FAITH. It is the assurance that comes only from Jesus, the author and finisher of it. Romans 10:17 says *So faith comes from hearing, and hearing through the word of Christ.* Faith is placing your complete trust and confidence in the Great I Am who can conquer every time. Faith is believing God's promises instead of what our circumstances and emotions are telling us in the moment.

When our Shoes of Peace are on, we are ready for the day. But if our faith is not continually being exercised, the peace that passes all understanding can still be momentarily stolen. The Shield of Faith is our weapon to diffuse or deflect the enemy's constant peace-stealing attempts. The faith shield is our fierce defensive weapon to use above all else against the accusing arrows of Satan.

Even though we have our "fuzzy slippers" on, the relentless one will still look for opportunities to rob us of our firm peace footing, just like he did with me at the beginning of this chapter.

When (not if, but when) arrows come, lift up your Faith Shield, either visually or physically. Then speak the Truth, "I trust you God. You are good and you've got this."

Lesson Learned:
Regardless of the circumstance or arrow,
lift up your shield and trust that God is bigger.

Helmet of Salvation

Put on salvation as your helmet... (Ephesians 6:17a, NLT).

SALVATION. It is the redemption or deliverance found only through the life, death and resurrection of Jesus Christ. Believers, we are covered by the blood of Christ. Debt fully paid. Fate eternally sealed. Christ lives in us. Period.

Just as sin entered the world through one (Adam at the Fall), both reconciliation and righteousness were granted through Another (Christ at the cross). This means *it is finished.* The evil one cannot steal your salvation. He will, however, do his best to make you question or doubt it.

The Helmet of Salvation protects us from Satan's life-stealing deception that occurs in the mind. It also reminds us of our security in Christ. Practically speaking, to put on our helmets means to renew our minds with God's Word, bind it to our foreheads and write it on our hearts.

When we put on our helmet, we are putting on the mind of Christ. Just as we have died with Christ, we have been raised to life just as He was. We are a new creation, therefore, it is no longer us living but instead Christ living within. To operate in the mind of Christ, our old nature or old fleshly attitudes and thoughts have to be evicted. As we do our part, the Holy Spirit will do His, bringing about heart change.

Lesson Learned:
If you start to question your salvation or God's promises,
recognize Satan's deception and retrieve your head covering!

Sword of the Spirit

...and take the sword of the Spirit, which is the word of God (Ephesians 6:17b, NLT).

THE HOLY SPIRIT. It is the active voice of God. Not only is He our constant Armor Bearer in battle, He offers comfort in mourning, encouragement in disappointment, wisdom in circumstances and strength in trials. John 14:26 says, He is our advocate who will teach and remind us of all He has said to us.

THE WORD OF GOD. Our weapon, according to Hebrews 4:12 (NLT), that is *sharper than any double-edged sword, it penetrates even to dividing soul and spirit, joints and marrow; it judges the thoughts and attitudes of the heart.* We use our sword:

- Defensively - to counterattack or cast out the enemy's lies
- Offensively - to strike against the enemy's advances through prayer
- Internally - to expose our innermost thoughts and desires

Ephesians 6:17 says for us to *take* or *wield* the sword. In Hebrew, take means to *receive* and *accept*. Taking up the sword of the Spirit is allowing Truth to penetrate our hearts as we seek out His voice. It's not being afraid to speak Truth in love when others need to hear it. It's also speaking against the enemy's direct attacks on Truth.

As an American, I have unlimited access to God's Word and must understand the responsibility of what I've been given. Believers, we need to ask ourselves daily the following, for this is how we take up our Sword:

- Am I continually *tightening* Truth - reading, studying, learning and sharing it with others?
- Am I *allowing* God's Word into my heart where transformation occurs?
- Do I *believe* what the Word says and receive its healing power?
- Do I *sift through* my thoughts and reject what is contradictory?
- Do I *speak* the Word aloud when the enemy attacks?

Lesson Learned:
Wield my sword and boldly proclaim what is true!

Cover Everything in Prayer

Pray in the Spirit at all times and on every occasion. Stay alert and be persistent in your prayers for all believers everywhere (Ephesians 6:18, NLT).

PRAYER. It is fellowship with our Father. Conversations with our Creator. Listening to and expressing love to our Lord. Presenting requests to our Provider. And sitting with our Sustainer. This may very well be the most rewarding and powerful weapon or treasure we possess.

Honestly, I used to skip over this last piece of my spiritual clothing. Not anymore. In fact, it's the most important piece because it holds everything together. Praying in the Spirit is the final step to procuring victory over the enemy. Omitting verse 18 from our armor ritual leaves us with an incomplete thought. We may be ready for battle, but we still need the Holy Spirit to walk it out.

As I think on this verse, I hear the word *constant.* What is our constant? It's the Holy Spirit; our constant Companion, Counselor, Guide, Intercessor and Strength who never grows weary. In order for His constant to shine through, we need a constant awareness of His presence and power.

Pray in the Spirit at all times, on all occasions. This command was hard for me to understand at first, because I pictured prayer as a continuous activity of me speaking. Our busy culture and the enemy's slight twisting have deceived many into believing praying at all times is physically impossible or an unrealistic goal.

Prayer is a two-way dialogue between you and God. This is Truth. It not only includes presenting our requests, worship and thankfulness to Him, but more importantly, listening to and being still before Him. A soldier stays in tune with his superior officer's instruction so he can step out in obedience when called. If we're too busy and doing all the talking, we will not hear the Spirit's prompting.

Our prayers often look different depending on our mindset at the time. For example, when I'm consumed with a worldly perspective, I pray for my life to become easier, for God to fix what I'm in and to be rescued from my circumstances. While this is not wrong because God wants to hear my heart, these prayers are often not in line with His perfect will. I have to remember He sees the bigger picture. His ways and thoughts are higher, and He knows what's best for me.

When we pray with an awareness of and a surrendered heart to His Spirit, we are praying with a God-focus and our prayers come into alignment with His will. This is praying in the Spirit and the posture needed to complete our armor ritual.

Lesson Learned:
Prayer is a two-way dialogue.
Listening may just be more important than speaking.

Conclusion

In Ephesians 6:10-18, the Apostle Paul calls all believers to be strong in the Lord and put on the whole armor. He then provides us with the how to. To see clearly and fight victoriously in daily battle, the armor must be present to:

1. Rid self of the "civilian life" – enslaved or worldly thinking
2. Seek God and what He says – Truth thinking
3. Step out in His power – not our own

Let's not go another day vulnerable, exposed and defeated.
Put on the full Armor of God so you may stand your ground.

BATTLE ORDERS
Ch 6 - God's Power

TAKE AWAYS

1.

2.

3.

REFLECTION: Wrestle with the following questions. Write out your answers in a separate journal, then discuss for clarity and accountability.

1. What steps do you take to mentally and spiritually prepare for your day?
2. Are you wearing God's Armor right now? If not, why? If yes, how can you tell?
3. What pieces of God's Armor do you find it difficult to put and keep on? Why?

BATTLE TOOL: Dress (Armor Up)

1. Meditate on Ephesians 6:11-18 and anywhere else the Lord leads about His power and protective armor.
2. Ask God to show you how to put on each armor piece.

3. What action steps can you take to form a daily habit of clothing yourself with God's power?
4. Do not go another day without God's Power. *You have armed me with strength for the battle; you have subdued my enemies under my feet* (2 Samuel 22:40, NLT).

Ex: Visually imagine yourself putting on each piece of armor as you describe what each is for and why you are putting that particular piece on.
Ex: As you are getting ready each day, take a part of your daily routine and associate it with a piece of your armor. Walk through it spiritually as you physically dress.

- Tighten the Belt of *Truth*
- Receive the Breastplate of *Righteousness*
- Put on the Shoes of *Peace*
- Put on the Helmet of *Salvation*
- Lift up the Shield of *Faith*
- Wield the Sword of the *Spirit*
- *Pray* in the Spirit

*Go deeper verses from this chapter: Matthew 19:26, Esther 4:14, John 3:30, 1 Corinthians 2:16, Romans 6:4, 5:18; 2 Corinthians 5:17, Galatians 2:20, Ephesians 4:22-24.

7

GUARD YOUR GATES

Do not be conformed to this world, but be transformed by the renewal of your mind, that by testing you may discern what is the will of God, what is good and acceptable and perfect.

— ROMANS 12:2

1988 BIRMINGHAM, ALABAMA

I sat in the wooden pews of my home church listening to the familiar hymns and the weekly Sunday sermon. This was when I heard my Savior calling. The preacher asked if anyone would like to be baptized, and if so, to come down the aisle. I didn't go though. I wanted to, but fear inhibited me.

What would people think? Everyone will stare. I'm too young. I'm too embarrassed. Am I really good enough to be baptized? These subtle assaults held me back, but only temporarily.

When the service ended, I told my mom I had wanted to go

forward. She took me to see my pastor and I was baptized a few weeks later.

Growing up, I wanted to be liked, to do the right thing, and for others to think I was this amazing person. *That's what being a Christian is all about, right?* It became my job to be perfect and not let anyone down. I'm sure you can imagine how that went.

I focused on my actions which distracted me from the inner accusations taking over my mind. *Christie, you've got to be better, nicer, prettier, thinner, smarter, more involved...* This exhaustive list went on and on and replayed each morning.

Different events overtime would feed my mind more negative messages, further confirming my inadequacies. I was blinded by my own unrealistic expectations and the following lies:

- *I'm not good enough, and therefore, unworthy of anything good.*
- *Christ's sacrifice saves me when I die, but I still need to make up for my failures and shortcomings now.*
- *I need to prove that God made a good choice when He picked me.*
- *If I try harder, then I can become good enough.*

These faulty mindsets became my default thinking and contaminated my life. Even when I started recognizing the lies, I was powerless to change my belief in them because the noise was too loud and the feelings too strong.

The Mind

Blinded by what is seen. Enslaved to wrong thinking. These are not God's good plans for us. How do we become so sidetracked and veer down roads of such toxicity? *I'm not good enough.* This was my inner song that was set to repeat. What catchy phrase consumes you? Listen carefully, and you will likely hear a theme you live by.

The thief has come to steal, kill and destroy, and his battleground is our thought lives. This ferocious lion spoken of in 1 Peter 5:8 is roaming and our gates, the space between our ears, have been compromised. Believers, this is an invasion and it's time we do something about it. We are the gatekeepers of our minds.

Are we to blame for every thought that comes into our mind? I don't believe so; however, we are accountable for what we do with each thought. What we allow to remain in our mind is our responsibility. If we want daily victory, we have to protect our gates, guard our thoughts!

Satan will succeed in his mission against us only to the degree we let him affect our thoughts, perceptions and beliefs. He knows if we think on something long enough, we will eventually believe it and allow it to reside in our heart. Once a message reaches our heart, it plants its roots deep; and every time a belief is reaffirmed by a thought, the root further entrenches itself.

The Word

Satan's goal is to fill our minds with lies so the Truth doesn't reach or stay in our hearts. Dictionary.com states a lie is any false statement made with intent to deceive, or an intentional untruth. Simply put, a lie is anything that disagrees with Truth.

> *All Scripture is inspired by God and is useful to teach us what is true and to make us realize what is wrong in our lives. It corrects us when we are wrong and teaches us to do what is right* (2 Timothy 3:16, NLT).

Satan knows when we take hold of something untrue and allow it a place in our mind, he will gain the ground needed to steal, kill and destroy the roots of God's Word embedded in our hearts. God's Word is our only absolute Truth. Every thought that doesn't line up with scripture needs to go.

Learning to override the assault on our minds is part of the believer's mission and the key to strategy living. It is an offensive approach in that you become intentional in your thinking and perspectives. It is also a defensive approach by which you counterattack Satan's deceptive tactics with God's Word.

Someone else's faith cannot carry us; therefore, we must know Truth for ourselves. Some lies can be ever so slightly bent and unrecognizable unless a specific scripture is found to contradict it. Some lies are simply Truth taken out of context. We need to know the Word to catch this deception, and knowing the Word only comes by remaining in it.

The Truth

Many times, as Christians, we think we know scripture because we've memorized it. Unfortunately, just because we've memorized a scripture doesn't mean it has reached our hearts. We can know the Word in our mind, but not sincerely trust and believe it. The Word penetrates our hearts when it becomes bigger and more important than our thoughts. Only then has God's transforming Word reached our heart.

Why is this so hard? Because false beliefs have been allowed a higher place than God's Word, hardening our hearts to Truth. In order for Truth to become a sound belief, thoughts that conflict with it cannot remain. Truth can only be established in the heart once the false beliefs have been eliminated. It all starts with our thoughts. Whatever we choose to set our mind on for long enough will eventually become our truth, or default thinking.

THE MIND/COMPUTER CONNECTION

- A computer has a CONTROL CENTER we cannot see. Just like our minds, information goes through a series of input, processing, and then output. As our minds process thoughts and life experiences, we internalize them and form perceptions and feelings whether they are true or not. Beliefs are formed and then we act according to them.

- A computer has a DEFAULT setting or response it is programmed to. It relies on prewritten programs or factory presets. Our factory preset was given to us by the first man, Adam; and perceptions of our past have been written and continually updated by those old programs, or beliefs. We each have a default that was set into motion at the Fall. The world and our circumstances continue to feed into it. This is the way we view and respond to life experiences and our feelings.

- A computer can become COMPROMISED or "infected" with a virus through simply seeing, allowing or downloading corruptible content. Once contaminated, the computer either slows down to a mere crawl or is bombarded with constant popups, making the device barely function. For the device to work properly again, the virus must be removed. In Genesis when Adam fell, the virus of sin infected mankind. To this day, we struggle with the mind's thoughts, the heart's feelings and the brokenness of our bodies. The only solution to our problem is the perfect sacrificial blood of Jesus Christ that removes the believers' sin and makes them clean.

- A computer needs ANTIVIRUS SOFTWARE to prevent and protect it from further attacks. The device depends on this 24/7 protective software to prevent its gates from being compromised. Believers need a daily reprogram and protection strategy because we naturally default back to what we know, what we see or what's comfortable.

- A computer's default can be changed only if the USER instructs it to. We are the users and have the ability to choose right programming. This can only occur through reprogramming, restoring and renewing. Reprogramming, however, does require a "User" much stronger than ourselves. Looking back, I see now how my mind was so full of noise and lies that I was defeated before I started. When attacks came, I began to recognize them; however, no matter how hard I tried, I wasn't strong enough to change my thinking because I wasn't equipped. It is not humanly possible to switch gears without partnering with God and using the Sword of the Spirit.

A New Default

Setting a new default according to God's Word is what we need to protect our gates. Without it, our flesh and its feelings will eventually take over because that is what's been in charge for so long. God's Word is both our antivirus software and necessary programming. God's Word needs to continually be reinstalled, or updated, into our wandering minds.

> Do not conform to the pattern of this world, but be transformed by the renewing of your mind. Then you will be able to test and approve what God's will is—his good, pleasing and perfect will (Romans 12:2, NIV).

To have the strength to change our thinking in the moment of a spiritual attack, our mind must first be renewed. I repeat: It has to happen *before* the enemy's attack is even on our radar.

Renewing our mind takes a divine partnership. As we resist conforming to or copying the ways of the world, we are allowing God to transform us anew by changing the way we think. Transformation comes through doing our part and trusting God to do the rest. Setting a new default takes a re-training of our brains and it involves repetitive action of the following:

- Meditating on God's Word.
- Replacing wrong thinking with Truth thinking.

- Fixing our eyes on Jesus.
- Pleading for His strength and intervention.

Renewing our mind keeps our eyes fixed where they were meant to be, on God and not the world. Then and only then are we able to recognize and come against the spiritual assaults on our thought life. Being in the world but not conforming to its false messages is hard. In fact, living out our day and not becoming imprisoned by wrong thinking or false feelings is impossible in our own strength. It is only through the transforming work of the Spirit that our minds and hearts can be renewed.

Throw off your old sinful nature and your former way of life, which is corrupted by lust and deception. Instead, let the Spirit renew your thoughts and attitudes (Ephesians 4:22-23, NLT).

Did you catch the present-tense word "let"? While Galatians 2:20 says when we became a Christian, our old self was crucified; Ephesians reminds us we must continue to throw off that old self. Our old nature is no longer a part of us; however, we are in a habit of picking it back up. Why do we do this? Because it's our default. In a twisted way, it's our comfort, or what we know.

Satan loves to throw us the lines:

- *You will never change.*
- *It's just too hard.*
- *This is just who I am.*
- *Am I really saved?*

I have heard each one of these broken records. Thankfully, I now know the Truth. They are lies from the pit of hell. "I am a new creation! Not better or improved, but brand spanking new!"

We are responsible for throwing off our former way of life (negative thinking, false beliefs and destructive habits) and living in our new God-given life. We can step into this process by learning and believing what God says about sin, grace and how we need to lay everything down at the cross.

We don't need to change ourselves; we need to surrender to the One who can do it for us. We have to know the Word to understand God's plan for us and who we are in Christ. We have to become listeners and followers of His Word. Then, and only then, have we given the Spirit access to fully renew our thoughts and attitudes to His.

Lesson Learned:
We renew our minds; God transforms our hearts!

Renew Your Mind

Whether it's the distractions of the world, our flesh and its infantile ways or direct arrows from the flamethrower himself; our lives are full of interruptions. To renew means to resume an activity after an interruption.

> Think about it: You're watching a TV show on the edge of your seat and totally immersed in the plot. All of a sudden, the screen changes, followed by a long and obnoxious beep. "We interrupt this program for a very important message," is spoken and runs across the bottom of the blank screen.

You've been there, totally connected and feeling the storyline when all of a sudden, you're completely detached and caught off guard. In the same way, when we feel disconnection in our relationship with God, there has been an interruption, or an intrusion of our focus. While we cannot prevent life's daily interruptions, we can be proactive and prepared to cast them aside.

The "show" is our life and how it is intertwined with God's. We aren't just watching it. We are living it. We try to stay focused on Him and His story, but the interrupter likes to flash his "important messages" across the screens of our minds to distract. He can only succeed *if* we are caught off guard. If we're not prepared for an interruption, distraction is inevitable. Remaining on guard takes a *daily* renewing of the mind.

God promises transformation through daily renewing. While we cannot transform ourselves, we can allow God to transform us as we choose to think on what is true. Renewing is our part, transformation is His. It's a renovation of the mind; removing the old and broken, then replacing with the new and impenetrable. Just like renovating a home is a process, you must take one room and detail at a time. This takes time and commitment.

God is fully committed to doing His part.
Are you committed to yours?

Since God has made us all wonderfully unique, renewing our minds will look a little different given our specific interests, talents, and personality. However, they must all involve the Word of God and putting on His power. Renewing your mind is essentially tightening your Truth and putting on the Helmet of Salvation.

Lesson Learned:
Fill your mind with God's Word instead of the world's ways.

Increase your God Weight

Picture a balance scale measuring where your focus lies. One side represents how much we focus on the world. The other is our focus on God and His Word. I've learned if I'm not focused on God, then my focus is on the world. Clearly, in order to live for God each day, the balance must be weighted towards Him.

How can we become more weighted with a God focus?
Take a moment and consider this exercise.

Based on a life scale of 1 to 5, circle the number that best describes your current state in each category?

My MOTIVES for daily time with God:
An Item on my To Do List - 1 2 3 4 5 - My Lifeline

My FOCUS is on:
The world and self - 1 2 3 4 5 - God

My THOUGHTS are on:
My plans, ideas and feelings - 1 2 3 4 5 - God's Promises

My TIME is spent in:
Joy-Stealing ways - 1 2 3 4 5 - Life-Giving ways

I surround myself with the following RELATIONSHIPS:
Joy-Stealing - 1 2 3 4 5 - Life-Giving

For me, this was pretty humbling. However, it showed me areas I need wisdom in and help with. Remember your answers to this exercise. We will revisit this in our *Battle Order's* section.

Abandon Joy Stealers

Everyone has someone or something that steals their time and attention. Where or who are you spending the majority of your time with? Is there a specific activity or person in your life that takes your focus away from God? Take inventory of each day and learn how to identify and remove your joy stealers.

> I used to be addicted to celebrity gossip ("trash mags" and entertainment TV). This was a huge distraction for me. I even used to call it "my therapy" when I needed to get away. Personally, this practice was poisoning my mind and further entrenching my negative body image. Thankfully my husband canceled my magazine subscription as well as cable, and I'm finally recovering. Even today, when I'm in line at the grocery store amidst all the tabloids, it still takes everything in me not to become entranced, like an insect flying into a bug zapper.

Sometimes the places and people we are around aren't of our immediate choosing; but often they are. I've learned when I'm in a joy-stealing situation I cannot change, I must be intentional and find life-giving ways to spend the rest of my time.

Lesson Learned:
Seek out life-lines: healthy relationships and activities (i.e. serving others, getting involved in church, or listening to uplifting music).

Abandon Habit stealers

Often, we form habits over time that steal from us, whether in action, word or thought. An easy way to identify a habit is asking yourself what are the things that are hard to give up? Take inventory and identify life-stealing habits.

I wrestle with a habit of going to food for comfort, as well as, an overwhelming focus on and desire to be thin. As you can imagine, these two contradicting giants of mine constantly collide. The result is shame and feelings of failure. This recipe for disaster keeps me busy and downright exhausted as my abundance continues to be stolen. I'm enslaved not to one, but three nasty lies.

- *Food is my comfort instead of God.*
- *Thin is beautiful and what gives me worth.*
- *What I do and how I look defines me.*

When I'm not intentional, I will find myself constantly consumed with one or more of these lies. To interrupt my destructive thinking, I speak aloud the name of Jesus as well as relevant scripture. (i.e. 1 Corinthians 6:19 *I am a temple of the holy spirit... I am not my own.*)

Lesson Learned:
When our minds are renewed, we can interrupt
our destructive thoughts and habits.

The Gospel Default

Becoming more weighted with a God focus involves changing our defaults. What better mind default than the gospel. I've realized my soul needs to hear the gospel daily, like a broken record. Oh, but what a glorious record it is!

> "God loved me and chose me before He created the world. He proved that love for me by sending Jesus, who willingly came to take on my sin and die in my place. Jesus has given me His life, His righteousness, His strength and His standing without condition. I am forgiven. I am loved. I am His child. I am free!"

Wow! Speaking these words each morning transforms my day. My finite mind needs this daily dose of Truth.

Lesson Learned:
Hearing the Gospel daily is part of a successful renewing plan.

Renewing Rituals

Renewing your mind is a sacred practice of filling yourself with God and His Word. It is personal and unique to each individual. This holy activity between you a God should not be compared to others. Nor should it be determined by others. There are times, however, when we need to seek accountability from others when we fall out of our renewing habit.

I'm a creature of habit. I've found that if I do similar things each day to renew or keep a consistent schedule, I am more fruitful in all that I put my mind to. When I recognized the importance of hearing the Gospel daily and just how much God desires time with me, there was no question renewal had to become a daily ritual.

I discovered my renewing practices by trying different things, asking for God's guidance, and determining what activities drew me closest to Him. For me, it can look like a walk or jog in prayer, listening to worship music, sitting in "my chair" where I read the Word, a devotional or declare verses from my *Truth Binder*. My goal each day is to connect through prayer, His Word and humbly listening for His voice.

Renewing your mind doesn't have to be a huge "quiet time" production. In fact, this can be counter-productive. Unfortunately, Satan's deception keeps many from partaking in this life-giving strategy due to busyness or unrealistic expectations. If you look at your renewing tool the wrong way, it can become about performance instead of relationship.

Renewing your mind is not legalism or something to check off your to-do list. Renewing your mind is a relationship-building practice that brings abundance.

When our minds are renewed, we can identify deceptive thinking and we are equipped with His power to overcome. Renewing our mind is reminding ourselves who Christ is and what He came to do. It's about inviting Him into our day as Lord, Savior, Redeemer and Strength.

I have also learned I need "refills" throughout my day to remain powered up. I'm a morning person and I usually wake up ready to go. By mid-afternoon, fatigue sets in, bringing discouragement and other nasty arrows. Setting a noon or early afternoon renewal reminder on my phone reminds me to recharge *before* my weak moments.

Not everyone is a morning person. Don't worry, your renewing ritual should start when you wake up but doesn't have to be complete in one sitting. When you start your day, be sure to "get dressed," but then find those times when you are most alert and available to sit and listen. Then make a standing appointment. Show up and He will show you what this sacred time looks like.

Lesson Learned:
Renewing our minds is the difference between life and death in our day.

Conclusion

For to set the mind on the flesh is death, but to set the mind on the Spirit is
life and peace (Romans 8:6).

Renewing our mind is a vital step to choosing life and winning the daily battle. A mind set on the flesh is not strong enough to overcome spiritual attack. If we're not Spirit-focused and filling our minds with God's Word *before* the attack, essentially we're choosing to put our old nature back on like a coat and hope for the best. With this plan, because of our flesh, the enemy's tactics and the world's pull; we will eventually fail. Life comes from a moment by moment, Christ-centered focus.

Forming this lifesaving habit takes a daily commitment of surrender. Take the time to learn and experiment with mind-renewing activities. No matter what, don't give up. This gets easier with time and God will guide you in forming this life-giving habit.

Only with a renewed mind can you reclaim your thoughts
and move forward in *The Believer's Battle Strategy.*

BATTLE ORDERS
Ch 7 - Guard Your Gates

TAKE AWAYS

1.

2.

3.

REFLECTION: Wrestle with the following questions. Write out your answers in a separate journal, then discuss for clarity and accountability.

1. What thoughts, words, or actions are you programmed to wake up to or fall back into when life gets tough?
2. What thoughts, habits or activities steal your joy and peace? What is one change or positive habit you can implement to replace what steals?
3. Describe your quiet time with God. Are your expectations realistic and intimate, or legalistic and overwhelming. What lie(s) might you believe about this sacred time?
4. Revisit the life Scale exercise in the Increase your God Weight section of this chapter. What areas do you feel God leading you to grow in? What action can you implement to begin drawing closer to God in each area?

BATTLE TOOL: Renew (Set a new default)

1. Clear your mind of what your time with God is "supposed" to look like, and instead ask Him to show you. Sit with Him and write down what He reveals.
2. Try out different practices such as devotionals, walks, sitting still, listening to worship music, reading His Word, drawing, etc. Start with activities you enjoy or bring you closer to Him. Invite Him into your activities.
3. Be sure to always include His Word and put on His power (Battle Tool Chapter 6). Avoid religious rituals that feel like a chore instead of intimacy. Let Him lead you and customize this time.
4. Write out your renewing plan and implement it every day for one week.
5. Record any changes in thoughts, perspectives or feelings that begin occurring as you implement your renewal plan. Allow God to tweak as needed.
6. Make mind-renewing a daily life habit. Get comfortable with this tool before moving forward in your strategy.

8

CHANGE YOUR THOUGHTS

For the weapons of our warfare are not of the flesh but have divine power to destroy strongholds.

— 2 Corinthians 10:4

2006 Charleston, SC

You're failing. You're weak. You will never change...

Mental torture which started as spiritual jabs from the enemy were quickly becoming self-induced. A barrier was forming and I felt separation from God. Even my attempts to pray and read God's Word started to fail.

I thought if I could just hide from being me or quiet the inner-bully, maybe then I could find some relief. I started binge watching a TV series as different from my life as possible, and my screen addiction began. The thing with addictions is that the "drug" will bring relief for a moment, but before you know it, it's not enough and more is needed.

Unfortunately, I couldn't escape anymore with just one screen, so I added another. I would play online games on my iPad as I watched TV. Occasionally my iPhone would offer a third simultaneous outlet. Technology continues to evolve providing more devices (faster and better) to add to our digital cocktails. Pretty soon, no amount of screen time offered the relief I needed.

My pit was dark, but God was there. He began to whisper "All you have to do today is spend time with Me. I will take care of the rest." Despite the commotion competing for my attention, His still small voice continued to call, bringing with it hope.

I finally forced myself off the couch and began to "show up" for the only thing that mattered–my daily appointment with God. I reversed my old script with this new thought. "The only thing I have to do is spend time with you. God I will trust you with the rest."

With my infant son fastened in his stroller, I finally stepped out my storm door. "God, help me form a new life-giving ritual!" I walked and prayed. I began to fill up a spiral notecard binder with scripture after scripture God was speaking to me in my studies. My *Truth Binder* came with me on every walk. It became my ammunition and lifeline. Each day, I would force myself to do this one task – walk with God, flip through my binder and meditate on His Promises. I even began speaking my verses out loud and taking ownership of them.

I will not be afraid or dismayed at what lies ahead, for the battle is not mine. God it's yours! (2 Chronicles 20:15, NLT).

You promise to strengthen me! You will help me. You will hold me up with Your victorious right hand. (Isaiah 41:10, NLT).

Over time, God's Word began to flood my heart. The barrier vanished and the fog-like oppression cleared. I began to recognize the enemy's attacks and speak my scriptures against them when they occurred. My eyes were opening and in came God's strength and perspective.

Restore Your Thoughts

Renewing your mind is putting on a Kingdom focus and filling yourself with Christ before you even start your day. This practice is vital to winning the battle, regardless of your current emotional state or circumstances. A believer with an unrenewed mind is like a soldier unprepared for his mission, or a student walking into a quiz. When you are unprepared; anxiety, forgetfulness and confusion rise up and in comes defeat. Equally, when you are prepared, you exude confidence, strength and peace. Success most often follows.

The renewing process takes time, tweaks and occasional changes as God transforms you. There were times when I would just go through the motions and feel nothing. But I continued anyway because the Truth was I needed it. Be patient with yourself and stay the course as He personally teaches you this daily life-giving technique. Remember, the only thing you have to do today is *come*. Show up for your standing appointment with your Heavenly Father and watch His plans unfold.

Only when our minds are renewed can we identify and defeat spiritual assaults. We have a choice in what we think on and who we allow into our gates. I repeat: We can choose right thinking especially if we are prepared to. Just because a thought enters our minds doesn't mean it's true or that we have to keep thinking on it. We get to choose what we think about. God gave us free will, and this includes the choice of what to do, say and think. What great news!

Choose Your Thoughts

You are the gatekeeper of your mind. You get to choose what you think about. This means you are fully free to accept a lie, or wrong thought, as true and allow it to come into your mind to dwell. This also means you can cast out the falsities that steal, kill and destroy, by choosing to think on what is true.

If a thief came to your doorstep and knocked, would you let him in? Of course not. If he tried to force his way in, would you open it?

Obviously, you'd choose to protect yourself and resist him by slamming the door shut. What if there was a squatter already dwelling or a guest who was no longer invited? Wouldn't you take the necessary steps to vacate who doesn't belong?

The same action is needed at the gateway of our minds. Once we recognize the thief, the thought or the attack; we must take protective and resistant action by rejecting the wrong thought and seeking God's Word for the Truth. You are the "security guard" who waits at the gate and monitors what comes in your mind; and you get to slam the door on any thought you don't want to think on. You are also like an attorney fishing out lies already residing through self-interrogation. Or even a high school English teacher grading a non-fiction paper determining fact from fiction, truth from lies.

Eliminate Lies

> We destroy arguments and every lofty opinion raised against the knowledge of God, and take every thought captive to obey Christ, (2 Corinthians 10:5).

The Bible says we are to take *every* thought captive. This is how we fight for the life Christ died to give. The Word is our weapon to overcome the mental arrows of human reasoning, false arguments, rebellious thoughts, presumptions, accusations and lofty opinions. Anything that sets itself up against knowing who God is must be torn down.

Since the attack is in the mind, we must battle in the mind. I've learned this is a two-step process. First, take each thought captive. Every. Single. Thought. And second, make sure each thought obeys the Word, Jesus who became flesh. Our weapons are not of this world and can have massive impact if used correctly.

STEP 1: TAKE EACH THOUGHT CAPTIVE

Many people only do the first step, taking a thought captive. They change their thinking. Many New Age philosophers, self-help books and secular counselors say "change your thinking, change your truth." This imparts the false message that you can create your own truth. There really is no bigger lie because God's Word is the only absolute Truth.

> For example, *I am a bad person* changed to *I am a good person who deserves (fill in the blank)*, leads to positive thinking but it is still deception.

Doing only step one is not an option, because it rarely points you back to Truth. Asking God what He says about each identified thought protects you from being further deceived. It is easy to replace a negative lie with a positive lie. In only thinking positive, we may start feeling better; but we may also be taking in another lie and in return moving further away from God and His best.

Instead of battling with the Word, which is sharper than any double-edged sword, applying step one only is like picking up a butter knife to fight with. It is deception, just in a prettier package. You cannot call it Truth unless it is Truth and there is only one Truth – the Word of God. What God says is absolute. It's finished. Everything else is an untruth or empty thinking.

> *When the unclean spirit has gone out of a person, it passes through waterless places seeking rest, but finds none. Then it says, 'I will return to my house from which I came.' And when it comes, it finds the house empty, swept, and put in order. Then it goes and brings with it seven other spirits more evil than itself, and they enter and dwell there, and the last state of that person is worse than the first. So also will it be with this evil generation"* (Matthew 12:43-45).

Here, Jesus warns us what happens when we only do step one. Once a thought is taken captive and removed, another thought will come in and occupy that empty space (either Truth or another lie). As previously mentioned, there are thousands of thoughts constantly flowing through our minds. We must be intentional to make sure the replaced thought is based on God's Word. Anything else is false. Jesus warns the longer we allow this type of deception, the worse off we will be and the harder it is to break the chains of that false belief.

> Take my *not good enough* thought mentioned earlier. Is this thought true or false? It depends on who you're asking. The world says, "If you work hard enough you will be good enough." It also says, "Look out for number one (you)," which basically means you already are good enough. In fact, you are the best! These are two conflicting messages, and neither are true. If I don't know what God says and fill my mind with His Word, then I will merely be worse off than before without even realizing it.

Now, shift your thinking to a Kingdom perspective, which proves this thought is half true but one the enemy can use to completely rob you. Romans 3:23 says: *All have sinned and fall short of the glory of God.* This means no one is good enough.

This is Truth, but not the whole story. You can't stop there, because God also says in Romans 8:1, there is no condemnation for those who belong to Christ; and, in 2 Corinthians 5:17 and 21, we are a new creation. Because of His sacrifice alone, we are a new creation that receives His righteousness and not our own. We are good enough in Christ alone. This is something we have to receive, not earn.

> God already knew we could never be good enough,
> which is why He sent His Son to be our good enough
> and fully cover our not enough.

> If my mind wasn't renewed and if I wasn't meditating on the Word, I would not be able to see the repercussions of allowing this deception to remain. I would also not be able to identify a more positive lie. In fact, this is what I did for a long time. Even today, this lie tries to creep back in when my mind is empty or not renewed. If I do not stay on

guard and spiritually dressed, I can fall back into a performance, works-based type of wrong thinking.

Lesson Learned:
Deceptive thoughts must be removed and replaced with only what is true.

STEP 2: REPLACE LIES WITH TRUTH

The only way to form a habit of right thinking is to know the Word of God and learn how to use it as your weapon. I'm amazed how quickly I can lose focus and forget the power of His Word.

- God's Word is Direct Instruction

All Scripture is breathed out by God and profitable for teaching, for reproof, for correction, and for training in righteousness, (2 Timothy 3:16).

- God's Word is Undefeatable

For the word of God is living and active, sharper than any two-edged sword, piercing to the division of soul and of spirit, of joints and of marrow, and discerning the thoughts and intentions of the heart (Hebrews 4:12).

- God's Word does not Return Void

So shall my word be that goes out from my mouth; it shall not return to me empty, but it shall accomplish that which I purpose, and shall succeed in the thing for which I sent it (Isaiah 55:11).

Fight with the Word

The Apostle Paul wrote the book of Philippians while imprisoned, yet he didn't allow his thoughts or environment to consume him. In fact, he was burning with a passion to encourage Christ followers with a letter of joy – the Truth.

Wow! What a testimony. The physical circumstances and the arrows Satan hurled could not keep him from the Truth and his mission. My friends, we have that same Power and double-edged Sword at our disposal.

> *Finally, brothers, whatever is true, whatever is honorable, whatever is just, whatever is pure, whatever is lovely, whatever is commendable, if there is any excellence, if there is anything worthy of praise, think about these things* (Philippians 4:8).

How do we protect our mind and wield our Sword? By sifting through our thoughts just like a water filter sifts through and casts out impurities. Test each thought against Philippians 4:8 and determine: Is your thinking True? Noble? Right? Pure? Lovely? Admirable? Excellent? Praiseworthy? Notice the first requirement is Truth. If your thoughts do not line up with Truth, cast them out, because they are not from God.

Feast on the Word

> *Your words were found, and I ate them, and your words became to me a joy and the delight of my heart, for I am called by your name, O Lord, God of hosts* (Jeremiah 15:16).

In order to know what is true, God's Word has to be our daily nourishment. Just like our bodies need nutrients from healthy food to make us stronger, our souls need the nutrients of Truth thinking. Our part is to consume and digest His Word continually; His part is to absorb it into our being. Renewing our minds with His Word, as He transforms our hearts. Only then can we eliminate our infectious thinking.

We have a *Truth Filter*. It's the Holy Spirit who lives within every believer. Ephesians 1:14 says He is our deposit guaranteeing our inheritance in Christ. The Holy Spirit is our Helper, Comforter, Advocate and Intercessor; and he is on call 24/7 waiting and ready to help us distinguish Truth from lies. John 14:26 promises, He will teach all things and bring remembrance of Truth.

The Holy Spirit is also a gentleman. He never forces and always allows us to choose what we want. We must learn the Word of God and renew our minds with it. It must first be in our mind for Him to bring it back to our recollection. This is why we must continually seek out and meditate on God's Word.

> So Jesus said to the Jews who had believed him, "If you abide in my word, you are truly my disciples, and you will know the truth, and the truth will set you free" (John 8:31-32).

Replacing death with life, or lies with Truth, is everything. It's what equips and sets us free. Identifying our thoughts, casting out what is false and replacing with what is true. It's a process that takes training and gets easier as you abide in Christ, and come to know more and more of Him and His Word.

> My child, pay attention to what I say. Listen carefully to my words. Don't lose sight of them. Let them penetrate deep into your heart, for they bring life to those who find them, and healing to their whole body (Proverbs 4:20-22, NLT).

If a soldier leaves his weapon at base camp and walks into battle without it, there could be catastrophic consequences. Your weapon won't do much good if it's left at home collecting dust on a shelf. Your mighty weapon isn't just a physical book. It's the living and active contents of the Bible that our minds must be fixed on so the Word can penetrate the heart. Deuteronomy 11 speaks of tying God's word as symbols to your hands and binding them on your foreheads. The *Believer's Battle Strategy* suggests collecting His word in a Truth Binder and arming yourself for the day. The Word is your weapon; wield is wisely!

Lesson learned:
Keep God's Word (your ammo) on hand and around at all times.

Speak So You Hear

Identifying our thoughts, casting out wrong thinking and replacing it with Truth thinking; what better way could we show our enemy we mean business than through Truth speaking? When we choose to boldly speak God's Word aloud, it takes our strategy and the results to a whole other level.

> *A small rudder on a huge ship in the hands of a skilled captain sets a course in the face of the strongest winds. A word out of your mouth may seem of no account, but it can accomplish nearly anything—or destroy it!* (James 3:4-5, MSG).

Whoever came up with the children's rhyme "Sticks and stones may break my bones, but words can never hurt me" wasn't listening to their Truth Filter. I see how the intentions behind it were good; but talk about planting deception in a child's life early on and creating a belief that can do horrendous damage.

> *Death and life are in the power of the tongue, and those who love it will eat its fruits* (Proverbs 18:21).

Our words have the power to bring life or death. James even compares the tongue's power to a rudder controlling the direction of a ship. It all comes down to what we say, whether to ourselves or others. While we can't control other's words, we can control what we say.

> Words spoken have power over our minds. Right now, think about anything but a "red apple." Can you think of something else or are you seeing that red apple? Now, think about a "yellow banana" instead. Is the apple still there along with the banana or have you moved on to picturing the new object? This time, speak aloud the name of the object – "watermelon." Which was a more powerful way to switch the direction of your thoughts, thinking it or speaking it?

> *So faith comes from hearing, and hearing through the word of Christ* (Romans 10:17).

We will believe what we hear. God gave us His Word so we can know and believe it, therefore we need to hear it and often. Who do you hear the most? It's yourself. In fact, you can't get away from yourself. Whatever you say, you are listening to, and eventually will believe.

Is it you speaking, or words spoken over you? Are negative words constantly present? Whatever words you are listening to, you will ultimately believe. What you believe will proceed from your lips and manifest in your life. This is why the Word of God must be written on our hearts. Speaking the Word aloud is a posture that speeds up this process.

Lesson Learned:
Speak God's Word aloud so we hear it, learn it and come to believe it.

Speak So The Enemy Hears

God's Word, our double-edged sword, is used offensively against our flesh by exposing our innermost thoughts and desires. God's Word is also used defensively against our enemy who wages war on us.

We've already determined Satan is a created being. He seeks to deceive in the mind by hurling flaming arrows in the form of wrong thoughts. Even though all of this takes place in the mind, there is no evidence Satan can hear our thoughts. God is the only one who is all powerful, all present and all knowing.

Why would we even chance the enemy not hearing us proclaiming Truth over his darts of deception? Even Jesus, in Luke 4, spoke against the enemy's attacks on Him. And what did He say? He quoted scripture every time. We will revisit this part of the story in a later chapter. But for now, we need to understand Jesus came not only to be our Substitute, but also our Example to follow. That's enough Truth for me to take a posture of speaking the Word against my enemy.

Coming from a conservative religious background, speaking the Word aloud was awkward for me at first. I asked myself why and heard the following thoughts:

- *What would people think?*
- *Will I become a Jesus fanatic?*
- *Is it really necessary?*

Who are these messages coming from? I knew it wasn't God, so it had to be the enemy. I trusted the process, remained persistent and have seen the transforming power of speaking God's Word. I now speak His Word whenever and wherever I need to hear it. Do not let the enemy steal this treasure from you.

Lesson Learned:
Speak the Word of God out loud
and break the power of the enemy in your life.

Conclusion

Replacing lies with Truth comes by deciding ahead of time to renew your mind by leaning on your Truth Filter. It also takes a deliberate choice to create a new habit. Take time with this concept and persevere as your spiritual muscles strengthen. This practice can become second nature with repetition. Continue in this posture and form a life habit that will follow you well beyond the completion of this book. Your life, or the quality of it, depends on strategy living.

The foundation of *The Believer's Battle Strategy*:

TAKE LIES CAPTIVE

+

REPLACE WITH TRUTH

+

DECLARE TRUTH

=

FREEDOM FROM ENSLAVED THINKING

BATTLE ORDERS
Ch 8 - Change Your Thoughts

TAKE AWAYS

1.

2.

3.

REFLECTION: Wrestle with the following questions. Write out your answers in a separate journal, then discuss for clarity and accountability.

1. For a week, identify and write down the following: First, your thoughts and feelings about your past, present or future. Second, what you say about yourself, others and your circumstances. Third, what others say about or are speaking over you.
2. Filter these findings through Philippians 4:8. What lies can you identify?

Finally, brothers, whatever is <u>true</u>, whatever is honorable, whatever is just, whatever is pure, whatever is lovely, whatever is commendable, if there is any excellence, if there is anything worthy of praise, think about these things (emphasis mine).

BATTLE TOOL: Replace (Eliminate Lies with Truth)

1. Identify lie(s) from reflection. (Ex lie: *I'm not good enough*)
2. Discover the root or heart issue. What am I feeling? (Ex Root Issue(s): Doubt, fear/anxiousness, condemnation)
3. Locate scripture to combat false thinking. Use a concordance, bible app or the internet to search scripture based on the life stealing "roots" you discover.

- *There is therefore now no <u>condemnation</u> for those who are in Christ Jesus* (Romans 8:1).
- *Do not be <u>anxious</u> about anything ...* (Philippians 4:6-7).
- *For our sake he made him to (Christ) be sin who knew no sin, so that in him we might become the righteousness of God* (2 Corinthians 5:21).

4. Record scripture in your Truth Binder.
5. Speak aloud scripture against the lie *before* and *during* the attack for you and the enemy to hear.

- *"There is no condemnation for <u>me</u> because <u>I</u> belong to Christ Jesus.*
- *<u>I will not</u> be anxious about anything, but in everything, <u>I will</u> present my requests to God with thanksgiving, and God's peace will guard <u>my</u> heart and mind in Christ Jesus.*
- *<u>I</u> have already been made right with God through Christ."*

9

THE POWER OF CHOICE

I call heaven and earth to witness against you today, that I have set before you life and death, blessing and curse. Therefore choose life, that you and your offspring may live,

— Deuteronomy 30:19

New Year's Resolutions

Tomorrow I will start exercising and eating right. I laid my head on my pillow ready for a new day and committed to the change I had chosen.

Day 1: I wake up extra tired and the lies start – *Just sleep in. Start tomorrow. You're never going to change anyway.* The first day of choosing a new habit is about as hard as a camel going through the eye of a needle. But I willed myself through, put on my tennis shoes and started forming my new habit.

Day 2: *Christie, you can do this!* Surprisingly, I force myself out of bed again and choose to do the exercise I've committed to. I have more energy than usual.

DAY 3: I wake up tired, but exercising is getting easier. *I really can do this!*

DAY 4: Throbbing muscles in places I didn't even know existed greeted me as my eyes opened. I was in pain, but I choose to work out anyway.

DAY 5: My body hurts so bad I don't even think I can walk. I sit up in bed and talk myself into skipping a day. I hit snooze on my alarm and roll back over to sleep. Out of routine, I walk out my door and forget my "spiritual clothes." Feelings of guilt and failure follow me through the day.

DAY 6: I don't feel like exercising today because *I've already messed up.* So, I choose not to and instead, go through a drive-thru and order a cheeseburger with fries. *I knew I couldn't change. It's hopeless,* I think as I supersize my meal.

DAY 7: My alarm buzzes right on time but I turn it off and go back to sleep. Unknowingly, I invite my old familiar lies back to stay.

CHANGE. It's easier said than done. I recently read an encouraging excerpt from Joanna Weaver's book that freed me tremendously:

> *Consistency is not perfection, it's refusing to give up.*
>
> — HAVING A MARY HEART IN A MARTHA WORLD

I know there is someone else who needs to hear that. I can't tell you how many times I've heard someone say, "You just need to be consistent," when I've sought to make a change. This statement always brought condemnation because my definition of the concept was all wrong. Consistency is not perfectly performing or abruptly stopping a specific action. Instead, it's refusing to quit trying even when we fail.

Consistency is enduring or staying on track and finishing the race God has set before you. We've reached the point in boot camp when things start to get physical. Or even more personal. It's inevitable that at times we will make wrong choices, but strategic living is learning how to utilize the Power God gives you to make the next right choice.

We are made in the image of God; therefore, we must understand the power we possess. God breathed His life into man alone, and out of love gave us free will. Even before Christ, while dead in sin, mankind was given the power of choice. With this gift comes responsibility. And ever since, we've dealt with an inner struggle regarding that power and responsibility.

Two sayings come to mind; *"Knowledge is power,"* and *"With great power comes great responsibility."* But instead of listening to Spiderman's Uncle Ben or historical figures, let's go to whose voice really counts; God's.

The wise prevail through great power, and those who have knowledge muster their strength (Proverbs 24:5, NIV).

But someone who does not know, and then does something wrong, will be punished only lightly. When someone has been given much, much will be required in return; and when someone has been entrusted with much, even more will be required (Luke 12:48, NLT).

Lesson Learned:
Our choices have the ability to bring ruin or restore life.

Whom Will You Serve

Believers, we are at a crossroads and can no longer stand still. In fact, we are now called to move forward, because if we don't, we're actually moving backwards. Moment by moment, we are presented with a choice. The choice to either turn away from the Truth revealed and place our trust in what is seen; or armor up and spiritually step into His abundance.

What we choose has significant ramifications. Deuteronomy 30:19 clearly states it; *I call heaven and earth to witness against you today, that I have set before you life and death, blessing and curse. Therefore choose life, that you and your offspring may live.* Let's break this verse down:

I call heaven and earth to witness against you today...

Do you see it? Both the physical and spiritual realms are called to be witnesses to our choices. There are spectators both seen and unseen; observing, here on earth, as well as in the great heavenly throne room as our prosecutor hurls out his accusations. What kind of choices will they witness in your life?

... that I have set before you life and death, blessing and curse.

Free will presents us with the freedom to choose what we want in this life, blessings or curses. As previously discussed, not every circumstance is a choice; however, the way we perceive and allow a circumstance to affect us is our choice. We can blame no one for our choices for they are ours alone.

God created us uniquely. We are tri-part beings with a spirit, soul and body. This means, we are both spiritual and physical, seen (body) and unseen (soul and spirit). God is a God of order, who designed us to live out of a hierarchy within ourselves (the body serving the soul and the soul serving the spirit). Allowing your spirit to take the lead and listen to His Spirit fulfills God's plan for you and brings about His abundance.

Our spirits, which are connected to His Spirit at salvation, were intended to guide both our souls (mind, will and emotions) and physical bodies. Unfortunately, when Adam and Eve fell, there choices resulted in spiritual death for mankind. The flesh then became the decision-maker and the spiraling process began.

We are born making choices based only on what is seen (i.e. past experiences, current circumstances, thoughts, feelings, assumptions, etc.) When someone accepts Christ, an inner battle to die to selfish desire and ambition occurs. We can win the fight by allowing our born-again spirits to take their rightful leading position.

... Therefore choose life, that you and your offspring may live,

Did you know what you choose to think, do and say not only impacts you, but the generations after you? A moment's choice will not only affect today, but tomorrow, and more disturbingly others who are looking up to you. If you have children, I'm sure this is eye-opening and doubles the stakes. A child picks up on the habits, choices and responses of their parents, and they begin modeling them.

If you do not have your own children, there is still a responsibility to the younger generation. We all have children in our lives whether family, friends' kids or neighbors, etc. We all have an impact on those who come after us. Let this sink in: Your choices matter. That's a huge responsibility, but do not let fear take hold. It is a responsibility the Holy Spirit is ready and waiting to help you carry *if* you allow him to – if you *choose* for Him to.

Choose Life

Life boils down to two decisions and a lot of choices. The decision for eternal life (accepting Jesus as your personal Lord and Savior) is a one-time resolution. Once this crucial choice is made, *it is finished.* No one can take your salvation from you, especially the powers of this dark world. The decision to experience abundance here on earth now is our second choice and it is a daily one.

Notice Deuteronomy 30:19 doesn't end with a complete thought. We now know we are to choose life continually, so how do we do this in such a complicated world? Verse 20 gives us our answer; *by loving the lord your God, obeying his voice and holding fast to him, for he is your life and length of days.*

> *The life I now live in the flesh I live by faith in the Son of God, who loved me and gave himself for me* (Galatians 2:20).

Choosing life daily means we choose Christ daily. We surrender what we think, trust what He says and allow Him to strengthen us. As Christ followers, we have died to our flesh and received a new heart. This newness is not a more improved us, but actually Christ, the perfect One, living within. We cannot claim responsibility for this change, it is only through His power and grace.

Believers, we have a new nature, but Satan likes to use our flesh, or our old ways of thinking and acting, against us. Our flesh has been in charge for so long, and the enemy wants you to believe it's still in control. Heart transformation can be a tough and painful process. However, it will happen if we remain focused on God, for it's *not by might, nor by power, but by His Spirit.*

How is daily surrender possible? Through strategic renewing of the mind. The more we renew, the stronger we become and the easier surrender will be. Seems overwhelming at first; but the more our spiritual muscles are worked, the more comfortable we will be in doing the action(s) we are called to.

Lesson Learned:
Do not worry about tomorrow;
instead, focus on Christ and do the next right thing.

Choose Your Perspective

Every day we have choices to make involving what we think, feel, do and say. These choices determine who, where and what we become. You are who you are today because of the perspectives, mindsets or beliefs you've chosen about what you've gone through.

This statement is not to downplay tragic or tough circumstances because there are so many in this broken world. Others may have made a choice that directly impacted you. However, regardless of what's happened, we have a choice in how we will allow each circumstance or event to affect us. We have the power to allow God to use what's happened for good instead of ruin.

Take two siblings who grew up with the same childhood experiences, yet as they grew older, resulted in completely different outcomes. One fell into substance abuse and ended their life, while the other became a social worker with a passion to help children in difficult circumstances. It happens all the time, and the big difference is perspective, the way we view what is happening. It all comes down to which lenses, or perspective, we choose to view life through; a worldly one or a Kingdom one.

A worldly perspective is one of self-focus, where our soul is in charge. It's the world's message and the way most choose to live because it is the human state and ingrained in us at birth. It's an "all about me and what I can see" approach towards life, where one allows their feelings to rule and determine the mental outcome and decisions of each day. When things are good, life's a party and we're the hero.

However, when things don't go our way, in comes self-pity along with a lot of other emotional junk. This was me for a long time and my life wasn't necessarily bad. Instead, my perspective of even life's common annoyances stole from me. I could only see what was physically going on, and hear the negative chatter stirring up in my mind. I allowed my feelings to control my thoughts and actions.

We are not meant to ignore our feelings, for they are real. Most often though, they are based either on false information or not taking into account all of the facts. Feelings are actually an indicator of what's really going on in our heart and, therefore, what needs to be addressed. However, our feelings are fickle, up one minute and down the next, sometimes without anything externally changing.

The majority of the time, our feelings are wrong and often get us into trouble. They only consider the circumstance and not God's Word. They don't allow the whole perspective or take into account God's promises or power. They are based on taking in just what is seen. We must choose to not *be like ships tossed around by the waves,* and instead anchor ourselves in Christ who never changes.

While a worldly perspective is soul-focused, a Kingdom perspective is Spirit-focused. It's choosing God's perspective instead of our own, His Truth over our feelings. It's recognizing our finiteness and God's sovereignty; and therefore, trusting He sees the whole picture and has our situation covered no matter what. My Take two scenario from Chapter 5 is a good example of how to walk out a Kingdom perspective during life's hiccups. A Kingdom perspective is choosing to live according to Truth, despite our circumstances or feelings.

Lesson Learned:
Pursue a Spirit-focused perspective.

Live Beyond Your Feelings

Why am I discouraged? Why is my heart so sad? I will *put my hope in God! I will praise him again – my savior and my God* (Psalm 42:5, NIV).

In many of the Psalms, King David expresses and addresses his feelings, yet chooses a Kingdom perspective despite them. Our mission is to do the same. When David was caught up in his circumstances, he chose to bring his feelings to God, surrender them and instead trust.

We must choose to be like the man after God's own heart; live by the Truth that sets us free, instead of our feelings that bring decay.

There have been plenty of times my feelings have tried to get the best of me. Many times, I cannot identify a specific thought, just a rotten feeling. This is a red flag alerting me something is wrong. It's an indicator to stop, take that feeling to God and choose Truth regardless of feelings.

For example, I will stop and pray aloud the following:

- "God, I feel sad, BUT I KNOW the joy of the Lord is my strength" (Nehemiah 8:10).
- "I feel empty, BUT I KNOW you are all I need" (Psalm 16:5).
- "I feel anxious, BUT I KNOW when I give you my concern, your unexplainable peace will guard my heart and mind in Christ" (Philippians 4:6-7).

Lesson Learned:
Live beyond your feelings by speaking God's promises.

Choose to Act

Do not merely listen to the word, and so deceive yourselves. Do what it says (James 1:22, NIV).

Thoughts and feelings eventually lead to action. Whatever is in our hearts will eventually flow outward. Soldiers are given orders they must obey, regardless of whether they understand or feel like doing them. Similarly, parents train toddlers up by directing them to act even if it's against the child's will. This directive technique is used for safety and to help develop reasoning capabilities so they may choose wisely as they mature. Their little brains are not aware or strong enough to act correctly without repeated guidance from their parent.

Allowing our Heavenly Father to direct our steps as our spirits mature is a must. This is part of our training. One way to allow God access is by surrendering our flesh to a repetitive action, or in other words, choosing a posture of submission in specific situations. This means making your flesh take a backseat and running to the Holy Spirit to do the rest.

If you're anything like me, my flesh often fights doing what's right or best for me. On the other hand, if it strangely wants to do what's right, it's because my flesh wants to have all the glory for doing it. Both need to be avoided. A posture of submission can help. Here are a few examples:

- When my flesh wants to sleep in an extra thirty minutes instead of spending time with my Lord which I know I need to get through my day, I can force myself out of my bed and take a posture of obedience; sit in a special place with God and my Bible asking Him to do what I can't. Just by showing up, I'm obeying and allowing Him to train me as the rest becomes second nature.
- When I know my body needs sleep and healthy food to fully live for Him tomorrow, I leave the temptation of late night TV and the pantry. I can take a posture of surrender and walk upstairs to read in bed.
- If I'm in a state of worry and can't move forward in something, I can take a posture of faith. I can fall to my knees and say the name of Jesus, or speak a specific scripture from my *Truth Binder*.
- When I'm walking through a tough season and the thought of choosing to do what I know I need to do seems

impossible, I can take a posture of humility and cry out for Strength, "Jesus help me!"

- When I'm not feeling strong enough on my own, I can take a posture and walk through a mind-renewing activity so my flesh will not have as much control and my mind will not be deceived.
- If I accomplish something I worked for and receive praise, I can take a posture of humility and immediately speak words of praise back to God instead of claiming it for myself.

Lesson Learned:
When we take an action step towards God,
He will carry us the rest of the way.

Choose to Believe

Truly I tell you, whoever does not receive and accept and welcome the kingdom of God like a little child [does] positively shall not enter it at all (Mark 10:15, AMP).

RECEIVE. ACCEPT. Welcome like a child. When I read this, I picture a toddler at the pool with his daddy. He is beaming with excitement and his eyes are locked in on his father. He takes his stance and jumps into the pool without hesitation because he knows his daddy will catch him. Believers, we are called to have this same kind of faith; a complete trust, confidence and belief in who God says He is and what He says He will do.

While our earthly fathers make mistakes, our Heavenly Father isn't capable of making even one. How much more should we trust Him? We have to believe that no matter what, if we're listening with eyes fixed on our Heavenly Father, He will catch us regardless of what He's calling us to do. And even if for some reason we take our eyes off Him for a moment, He will restore us if we humble ourselves. Do you believe this?

And this is the confidence we have toward him, that If we ask anything according to his will he hears us (1 John 5:14).

Rest assured, this child-like faith is God's will for us. Isaiah 43:10 declares we were chosen to know, believe and understand who He is. Therefore, speak the Truth aloud so you hear and come to believe the Truth. When we do our part, God will do His!

Lesson Learn:
Ask for an increased measure of faith, for this is what we were chosen for.

Choose to Receive

So much of the Christian life is about simply receiving the gifts Christ freely offers. Because we are so used to the world's way of thinking, this act of receiving is more difficult than it should be. The world says *Nothing is free. You have to strive to earn it.* Well, God's ways are opposite. What He offers is free.

For by grace you have been saved through faith. And this is not your own doing; it is the gift of God (Ephesians 2:8).

A shift in mindset from the world's ways to God's ways is needed. Choose to focus on the beauty of our precious and ultimate gift, Jesus Christ, for it is in Him that you have already been given *all the spiritual blessings in the heavenly realms.*

We can choose to forego these gifts simply by not receiving them. Paul, in Hebrews 4, refers to the Old Testament Israelites and their wilderness wanderings as our example:

> *God's promise of entering his rest still stands, so we ought to tremble with fear that some of you might fail to experience it. For this good news—that God has prepared this rest—has been announced to us just as it was to them. But it did them no good because they didn't share the faith of those who listened to God. For only we who believe can enter his rest. As for the others, God said, "In my anger I took an oath: 'They will never enter my place of rest,'"even though this rest has been ready since he made the world* (Hebrews 4:1-3, NLT).

The Israelites of Exodus chose to live without daily rest and abundance; and therefore, didn't receive God's promise of it. The same can happen to us if we aren't intentional in the choices we make. Let's learn from their mistakes:

- The Israelites placed their trust in what was seen in the moment. In order to receive an unseen gift, you must first believe it is there for you and then take hold of it. *God, open my eyes so that I may see!*
- What they believed poured out into their lives through complaining, impatience and doubt. Throughout the book of Exodus, the Israelites sought their own way, self-medicated and committed various forms of idolatry. *God, give me the power and desire to do what pleases You!*
- Instead of receiving the promise, hardened hearts and sinful actions led to a consequence (a lifetime of wandering in the wilderness). *God, direct my steps according to your Word.*

Did God break His promise to the Israelites? No. God does not waver in His promises, however, there are consequences to our actions. In this case, the promise was given to the next generation. This is sad, but also encourages me, as I think on my choices and how they negatively may or have already affected the generations after me.

For when I fail, I know God gently leads and His grace covers a multitude of sins.

Lesson Learned:
Despite our mistakes, we can trust God in all things,
especially with our children.

Conclusion

It's Christmas time. The lights are glowing and the scents of hot cocoa and cinnamon are flowing. Nestled under the sparkling Fraser Fir are beautifully wrapped gifts. There are more than you can ask for or imagine and each is labeled with your name on them. The gifts are yours. They always have been. Still, they aren't experienced until you:

1. Believe they are feely given to you.
2. Reach out (act), take hold of (believe) and open (receive) each one.

It's time. There are important choices to make. It's between our flesh (which is connected to the world and loves to be in charge) and our spirit (which is connected to God). What will you choose at this crossroad? Take steps forward no matter how small. The Holy Spirit is waiting for you to allow Him to bring victory. All you have to do is be a willing participant in His plan.

Oh, that you would choose life, so that you and your descendants might live (Deuteronomy 30:19b, NLT).

Choose today whom you will serve.

BATTLE ORDERS
Ch 9 - The Power of Choice

TAKE AWAYS

1.

2.

3.

REFLECTION:

YOUR PAST. List three life-changing events from your past.

1. How did you respond to the circumstances, thoughts and feelings present? What habit(s), if any, in thought, word or action caused further destruction?
2. Which perspective (Kingdom or worldly) did you choose to view each event through? If worldly ("all about me and what I can see"), go back and write down what a Kingdom (Spirit focused) perspective would've been in that circumstance. (For assistance, use my scenario examples from Chapters 4 & 5).

YOUR PRESENT. List three struggles or circumstances you are currently facing. Reflect on the same questions above in your current situation.

BATTLE TOOL: Choose (Live Life Abundantly)

FEELINGS VS. TRUTH EXERCISE.

Identify at least three negative feelings you've experienced recently and share them with the Lord. A Feeling Wheel (google) can help tremendously. Find scripture and choose to speak and believe Truth instead of your feelings. Make this exercise a habit when your feelings start to take over.

"I FEEL (feeling), but I KNOW (insert Truth)."

Ex: "I FEEL sad, but I KNOW the Joy of the Lord is my strength.)

CHOOSE TO ACT, BELIEVE AND RECEIVE

ACT: What weaknesses, moments and habits get the best of you during the day? What faith action or posture of submission can you intentionally take to keep a Kingdom perspective?

1. Implement your action plan each day this week
2. Ask for accountability from a battle buddy.
3. If the Lord tweaks your plan, let Him.

Ex: Early afternoon when I begin to feel tired and discouraged, I will stop whatever I'm doing and spend at least 5 minutes fully focused on Him, asking for His strength and renewing.

BELIEVE: Do you take God at His Word? All of it? Which of God's promises are hard to believe for yourself? Where is your doubt or hesitation is coming from?

1. Write down this promise in your *Truth Binder* and ask Him to increase your faith in it.
2. Speak aloud His word. Plead Mark 9:24: *"I do believe; help me overcome my unbelief!"*
3. Speak your promise often and trust your Great Provider for the rest.

RECEIVE: Have you received God's plan of abundance for you? Our part is to take a posture of surrender while pleading His Word one day at a time. He will do the rest. What posture (or action) is God calling you to take in order to fully receive? Reach out your hands and thank Him out loud in advance for this abundance Christ died to give you!

* Go deeper verses from this chapter: Genesis 2:7; 1 Thessalonians 5:23; 1 Corinthians 14:33; Zechariah 4:6; Ephesians1:3, 4:14; 1 Peter 4:8; Isaiah 40:11.

10

EXPOSING DARKNESS TO LIGHT

Again Jesus spoke to them, saying, "I am the light of the world. Whoever follows me will not walk in darkness, but will have the light of life."

— JOHN 8:12

2001 CHARLESTON, SC

The counselor's office felt safe and inviting. I'd come to discuss my food and body image issues, or at least that's why I thought I was there. Since I was getting older, I had to "fix myself" before I got married and started a family. It was crunch time.

I sat down on the floral cushions and the counselor asked me a series of questions. After I answered the final one, she paused and said, "Christie, you are depressed." My automatic response was, "You're wrong!"

A couple years later, in premarital counseling with my single's pastor, I was again asked if I dealt with depression. Again, I pridefully denied the presumption. Both meetings left me feeling defensive and embarrassed. But they also began to open my eyes.

Eventually, I came to terms with my reality. But, the thought of telling anyone my "secret" brought on waves of shame and fear. I'd worked so hard to be who others wanted me to be. I also worked tirelessly to hide the ways I fell short and the destructive practices I'd partake in to try and numb the pain.

I'm a Christian. I'm not supposed to struggle, especially in "this" way...

Believers, this is the part in our strategy that takes great humility and courage; a humbling of self to accept the true human state and having the guts to live out loud anyway. It takes an understanding of how once we were in spiritual darkness but because of Jesus we no longer have to be. He has called us out of darkness and into His marvelous Light. Out of sin and into forgiveness. Out of hopelessness and into abundance!

You are the light of the world. A city set on a hill cannot be hidden...In the same way, let your light shine before others, so that they may see your good works and give glory to your Father who is in heaven (Matthew 5:14,16).

We have been given Jesus, the Light, and are called to shine His radiance in this dark world. To walk as children of Light, we are to let Him shine through us in *all* circumstances. Not so we look perfect and portray an unattainable standard. Not so we can be lifted up for the good deeds we do; but instead, so others can see our need for the Savior, and how we allow Him to come in and transform us from the inside out.

Lesson Learned:
Be Christ's ambassadors by being a living testimony.

Children of Light

In Exodus, when Moses came down from Mount Sinai holding the Ten Commandments, he had to hide his face under a veil because the people were terrified by God's radiant presence. In Old Testament times the veil was necessary because Christ had not yet come.

> *So all of us who have had that veil removed can see and reflect the glory of the Lord. And the Lord—who is the Spirit—makes us more and more like him as we are changed into his glorious image* (2 Corinthians 3:18, NLT).

In New Testament Times, the veil can only be removed by receiving Christ, and thereby gaining freedom from the law of sin and death. As children of Light, we have been freed from our sinful thinking and actions as we surrender them to God for His glory.

I lost so much time deceived by the lie that I was supposed to get myself together *before* Christ could use or delight in me. New Testament living is not a life without sin. It's bringing out the darkness within us and exposing it to the Light above. It's calling out the father of lies and fixing our gaze on the Heavenly Father who restores and brings all things together for good.

We no longer have to hide. The Holy Spirit is the one transforming us little by little, and He who has begun this good work will bring it to completion. It's a promise, therefore, we can come to God just as we are and be used for His glory.

> *Therefore, since God in his mercy has given us this new way, we never give up. We reject all shameful deeds and underhanded methods. We don't try to trick anyone or distort the word of God. We tell the truth before God, and all who are honest know this* (2 Corinthians 4:1-2, NLT, emphasis mine).

This "new way" is our ministry; living the transforming process out loud so others can see the power of hope, forgiveness and restoration. All the shame and condemnation we've felt because of what happens to us or what we do is no longer valid because of Jesus' blood sacrifice. We are to tell the world of His great mercy through our stories and not keep them hidden.

Falling into deceptive thinking, acting like someone we are not, distorting the Truth and not displaying the real us; all of these things only "trick" others and point them towards darkness and hiding. Conversely, walking in humility points others to the Light. When you make mistakes or wrong choices, reveal it and watch God's Light shine through you as you share your struggles.

Lesson Learned:
Walking through confession and repentance outwardly
frees us from Satan's accusations.

Display the Truth

> *If the Good News we preach is hidden behind a veil, it is hidden only from people who are perishing...You see, we don't go around preaching about ourselves. We preach that Jesus Christ is Lord...For God, who said, "Let there be light in the darkness," has made this light shine in our hearts so we could know the glory of God that is seen in the face of Jesus Christ (2 Corinthians 4:3,5-6, NLT).*

When we screen and hide our stories, others remain blinded to God's redemptive power and grace. It is through vulnerability and humility that Jesus' light fully radiates through us and the veil is removed from unbelievers' eyes.

We must be so careful not to steal any of God's glory. That's the thief's way, not ours. When we hide our flaws and what God is doing inside of us, this is exactly what we are doing. It is through transparent living that God's Light, the gospel, is revealed. We are all sinners in need of our Savior and the world needs to know.

Lesson Learned:
When I hide the Truth, I am taking the focus
away from God and placing it on myself.

The Whole Truth

We now have this light shining in our hearts, but we ourselves are like fragile clay jars containing this great treasure. This makes it clear that our great power is from God, not from ourselves (2 Corinthians 4:7, NLT).

Let's face it, we are merely vessels. Without God we can do nothing, but with God we can do all things. As Christians, why are we to live our mistakes and struggles out loud? To show this broken world the only difference between us and them is Jesus.

We are not perfect nor were we meant to be. We are called to be conduits for unbelievers to see the unseen, Jesus' grace for all who believe. He is where our true peace, joy and assurance comes from. As we walk through struggles, our hope shouldn't remain in our self, others or circumstances; but instead, in the perfect One who lives inside.

And as God's grace reaches more and more people, there will be great thanksgiving, and God will receive more and more glory. So we don't look at the troubles we can see now; rather, we fix our gaze on things that cannot be seen. For the things we see now will soon be gone, but the things we cannot see will last forever (2 Corinthians 4:15,18 NLT).

Let's all take a moment and adjust our lenses. We lose focus when we fall into trying to be good or only showing our good. In doing so, Satan succeeds as we unknowingly try and take Jesus' glory for ourselves. Instead, we participate in Christ's suffering when we keep our eyes set on the unseen, what is to come and what will last.

Lesson Learned:
The Gospel is "seen" when we choose humility and transparency.

Transparency

Sharing your real story and being open and honest takes tremendous vulnerability. Have you ever done something so bad you feel if anyone knew about it, they'd never accept you? Or has something so horrific ever happened you felt no one can ever know? Do you feel that if people knew the real you, they'd turn and run the other way?

Our minds have been polluted with thoughts, beliefs and mindsets, twisted and molded by the prince of darkness so many times that sometimes we can't even see the Truth. Unfortunately, we are so full of shame and condemnation that we either keep the broken pieces of our hearts hidden out of fear, or we try to push them down and ignore out of pride.

We are too worried about what others think when instead we should worry about where others may eternally end up.

Do any of these thoughts run through your mind?

- *What would others think if they knew this about me?*
- *I can't show them who I really am.*
- *I have to keep this part of my life hidden; it's too shameful.*
- *I'm supposed to be a Christian.*
- *I don't need others' help. I can do this alone.*
- *I just want to be alone.*

Those, my friends, are lies from our accuser, and his plan to isolate. To isolate means to cut off from others. It happens to all of us and often it's so slow and subtle, we don't even see it until we are already broken, discouraged and alone. This effective tool of the enemy has an end goal to divide and conquer, keeping you from life-giving relationships so he can get the upper hand.

Then the Lord God said, "It is not good that the man should be alone;" (Genesis 2:18).

We are made for relationships. In Chapter 1, we talked about the importance of *battle buddies.* Listening and speaking Truth is one of their main roles. When you feel yourself hiding something, distancing yourself or taking offense, recognize the enemy's attempts to isolate. Fight back by being vulnerable and transparent with battle buddies.

Picture this: When an object is transparent, it allows light to pass through it so what's behind the object can be seen. Believers, we are those objects for light to pass through, vessels to be used for God's glory.

Transparency is our ministry. It's taking off our masks and being courageous and humble by letting others know the real us and what we are dealing with. This doesn't mean broadcasting our "stuff" to the world, but instead, having a trusted group of buddies to share the good, the bad and even the ugly.

However, your story was also meant to be heard and told to others with similar struggles. This is ministry. God brings all things together for good, so if you cannot see the good in what you've been through yet, you can trust God to use it for another.

Lesson Learned:
There will be times God prompts us to share our story
outside of our circle for His purposes.

Let God use your story for His glory

I've struggled with depression for over 24 years. The earliest I remember having symptoms was in college. I was good at hiding my struggle. I wore my "I'm great" mask when around others. Then kept busy and ignored it when I was alone. I denied it for so long. Regardless of people's proximity, I welcomed an isolated lifestyle.

My thoughts went something like this: *I'm a Christian. I'm not supposed to be depressed, or take any medication for it. I have to keep this part of my life hidden.*

In the Christian community, there is a difference in opinion on taking antidepressants. I am no expert, so all I can do is tell my story. For me, not taking the medicine hampered my ability to grow and be a light. Satan had me right where he wanted, paralyzed in darkness. I could not see my way out of the dark pit.

Eleven years ago, I realized I could not overcome this on my own, and not just spiritually. I finally confided in a friend who then opened up to me about dealing with depression as well. I felt instant relief because I wasn't the only one.

She asked me the question, "If you had high blood pressure or diabetes, would you take medication for those?" I said yes and it helped me understand why people take antidepressants. It didn't define me or where I stood as a Christian. It was medicine to help my body get back into balance, while I took my beliefs, mindsets and brokenness to the True Healer.

I started taking an antidepressant and all I can say is my life began to change. The fog began to clear. My "stuff" was still there, but, because the fog was lifting; I could see and face what was going on instead of trying to hide from it. Most importantly, my relationship with God began to grow exponentially. Who knew, a few years later I would meet Akoua in Togo, and the roles would be reversed. I would be the one to bring relief by sharing my story.

Sometimes, I struggle with shame that I still take medication. Out of pride I have tried to come off of my antidepressant or put a time limit on taking it. I've come to realize God is more interested in me being His Light than He is in me attaining perfection. I've had to surrender this part of my life. Antidepressants will continue to be a part of my story for as long as He allows.

Keeping my story secret not only hurts me, but also others around me.

- Choosing to be transparent with my *trusted friends* brings comfort, relief and spiritual growth.
- Choosing to be transparent with *others who are hurting* brings purpose and freedom.

Transparency is our Defense

Hiding from your "stuff" and not dealing with it locks you in a prison of your own doing. You can only put up a front and mask what is really going on for so long. Hiding is exhausting. You will eventually need respite. This causes you to isolate yourself even further until you're "strong" enough to put on your mask again.

When you share what you are going through, the enemy can no longer hold that thought, lie, sin or secret over you. He has lost his power because you've called him out and started the healing process. Now that I've realized this, any time I begin to struggle or have an irrational thought, I share it with someone. Try it. Experience this amazing sense of freedom and blow to the enemy!

> *For if they fall, one will lift up his fellow. But woe to him who is alone when he falls and has not another to lift him up... and though a man might prevail against one who is alone, two will withstand him—a threefold cord is not quickly broken* (Ecclesiastes 4:10,12).

There is strength in numbers, but be aware, isolation is not just physical proximity. Even if you surround yourself with people but only allow surface relationships, you are still isolating. We are made for relationships, not only so we can be a light, but so others can minister to us when we are weak. Do not allow the enemy to divide – it will result in defeat.

Lesson Learned:
Fellowship with others is part of our defense strategy.

Testimony is our Offense

There is tremendous pressure in being a woman today, from the way we look to what we do. Men face the same battles, only they look a little different. Unfortunately, the messages *put on a mask, appear perfect* and *don't let others see you struggling* cross genders and bombard us all constantly. We feel we have to fit a certain mold to be accepted, and we are constantly comparing ourselves to others.

Social media has only magnified this problem. The world's mold, and even the mold of the "perfect Christian" are Satan's ways of dividing. Wearing masks steals, kills and destroys, because they are not reality. While I can see behind my own mask, I can only see what you want me to and it leaves me feeling less than and not enough.

Do you have that friend who you strive to be like? Who seems to have the perfect life? What kind of feelings does that stir up in you (i.e. inferiority, discouragement, discontentment)? When you keep an "all together" mask on, you become unrelatable and are doing that very same thing to others. This sends the message that something is wrong with them, causing division and leading further into isolation. Do not allow the enemy to divide – it brings defeat onto others.

They triumphed over him by the blood of the lamb and by the word of their testimony (Revelation 12:11, NIV).

Believers, this is serious warfare and it works! Transparency through testimony is powerful and remains my passion and purpose. It is also a part of your purpose; don't let Satan tell you otherwise. Call him out. Tell others what you deal with. Let God use your story for His glory!

Lesson Learned:
There is someone who needs to hear your story.

Conclusion

We have become a mask-wearing culture. We end up putting on a front that everything is fine and we have things under control. If this is you, ask yourself; who is getting the glory here, you or God?

We fall into the trap of thinking the way to bring others to Christ is to act like we don't deal with things anymore, but unfortunately, this deception only pushes unbelievers and even some newer believers further away. If that wasn't damaging enough, consider this. When our best efforts to hide fail, which they eventually will, we are seen as hypocrites, often causing unbelievers to run even faster the other way.

We've all seen it happen. Could this be a big part of what's wrong in the church today? The world needs to see how we handle things. They need to see how we are still broken, but we take it to Christ, our Healer and Restorer. My friend, we all need to *see*.

To move forward in our strategy, we need to be honest with God, ourselves and others. Inner wounds (both ones we know of and those we don't) need to be uncovered so deception can be exposed, and healing can begin. The healing is of our heart, and it will take "heart surgery".

Yep, I said surgery, but there's no need to worry. Lift up your Faith Shield because your Great Surgeon has got this! Surgery is a process not to be taken lightly. Before it can take place, the patient must be triaged. This is a pre-op appointment where the specialist interviews the patient and compiles a complete list of symptoms and assigns a degree of urgency to the wounds or illness to target. Only then can the course of treatment be determined.

TRIAGE

This Chapter's *Battle Orders* are your triage appointment. In order for a successful surgery, we have to know and understand all that's going on. The *triage challenge* is to get as much of the noise that is consuming, deceiving and distracting you out and onto paper so you can see your situation clearly. The Great Surgeon already knows what He's dealing with, but this is the posture of action we take to allow Him to touch it.

Just as you prepare for surgery by fasting and emptying your stomach, you need to do the same through prayer and emptying your mind of all the noise. In other words, you must purge your mind of the painful experiences, destructive habits, negative feelings and irrational thoughts running rampant.

Anything that could be playing a part in stealing your
Spiritual Fruit must come out.

There's years of mental garbage to sift through, so be patient and push through. Don't let Satan steal the vital step of clearing your mind of his deceit. In giving this exercise, I've heard the objection, "If I write it down, then I'm agreeing with the enemy." This is a lie because if you're speaking it in your mind, you've already agreed with the enemy and it's affecting your life.

This posture of writing the lie out is actually calling the enemy out.
It's the first step of the purging process.

Physically exposing the mental garbage by seeing, reading and saying it aloud often opens your eyes and ears to how ridiculous, irrational and untrue these thoughts are. Once the lies have been identified and brought to the forefront of our minds, we can now do something about them.

It is only in secret (the dark) that Satan has power and control. When we allow secrets and lies to remain, our light is stifled and our abundance is stolen. Let's expose our enemy and his tactics to the Light.

Coming out of hiding is key to a winning strategy.
In fact, it's a game changer.

BATTLE ORDERS
Ch 10 - Exposing Light to Darkness

TAKE AWAYS

1.

2.

3.

REFLECTION:

1. DEFENSE: Who are your *battle buddies*? When you have an irrational thought or fear, when you sin or need help, don't isolate or hide. Instead, reject the secret or lie holding you captive by telling your battle buddy(s).
2. OFFENSE: Who outside of your circle is God calling you to share your story with? When God prompts you, step out in faith and watch Him both work through and bless your obedience!
3. MASKS: How do you hide or isolate?

BATTLE TOOL: Purge (The Triage Challenge)

Triage is critical. It is <u>not</u> meant to be glossed over, rushed through or a one-time exercise. Instead, it needs to become a necessary lifelong tool to identify mental garbage, tear down strongholds and prevent new ones from forming. Persevere through. I promise it gets easier the more it's practiced.

> *Behold, You desire truth in the innermost being, And in the hidden part [of my heart] You will make me know wisdom* (Psalm 51:6, AMP).

The best way to describe how I walk through this exercise is by looking at it like a puzzle you work on over time. My strategy is to create piles. The outer edge of the puzzle is completed first, and then the middle comes to life by working through the different sorted piles.

The following questions will spur thoughts, feelings, memories, etc. Write down *anything* that comes to mind. Accept the challenge of introspection and be intentional in creating space and time to record your findings, no matter what.

Only when you've purged and uncovered the noise in your mind are you ready for healing surgery.

Let the purging process begin! (Record your thoughts in a separate journal. Write down anything that comes to mind.)

1. Pick one new step each day to focus on.
2. Think on the questions asked and pray for clarity and courage.
3. Spend at least 10 minutes each day recording whatever comes to mind - no matter how silly, irrelevant or random. There are no wrong answers, you are just purging the junk. Use whatever journaling technique works for you (i.e. phrases, sentences, drawing, etc.) and cast perfection aside.
4. Be aware of the thoughts and feelings coming to the surface throughout your day. Go back and record your findings.

Triage has to happen *before* the infection can be treated.

When implementing this tool, stay protected. Keep your
Battle Tools close and the Holy Spirit even closer.

This process can be grueling, so don't go it alone. Invite God to go with you into these painful places to identify negative feelings and thoughts. If you get stuck in an area and don't feel you can move forward, reach out to friend, seek prayer at church or in small group, or consider making an appointment with a Christian counselor.

STEP 1: EXPOSE YOUR FEELINGS. Identify specifically what you are feeling. A Feeling Wheel (google) can help tremendously in this process. Let these questions open your eyes to what you are feeling. Write down anything that comes to mind.

1. How do you feel about exposing your feelings? Why do you feel this way?
2. Think back on your past week. What thoughts or feelings can you identify? What was happening in those moments and why do you think you felt this way?
3. What thoughts go through your mind when you become frustrated, overwhelmed, stressed, discouraged or just bored?
4. During your day, when do you feel yourself losing your peace or joy? Explain.
5. Can you identify a common trigger (i.e. a specific time, place, action or person) that brings on negative feelings?
6. Pray the following prayer. Afterward, sit quietly with him and write down anything more He reveals.

Father, forgive me for living by my feelings. I know they are not what's true, however, they are mine and I bring them to You to show me what's true. Jesus, you came to heal my heart and bind up my wounds. I allow You full access to my feelings. Give me eyes to see how Satan is attacking me in this area and the grace to expose his plan through my writing. Thank you in advance for your protection, revelation and healing. In Jesus' name, Amen.

STEP 2: EXPOSE YOUR THINKING. Thoughts are constantly running through our mind. Many are re-occurring subconscious ones about our past, ourselves, others or our circumstances. If we hear these thoughts long enough, we will believe them and accept them as true. This becomes our inner dialogue or self talk. Let these questions open your eyes. Write down anything that comes to mind.

1. What thoughts, no matter how random, run through your mind?
2. What do you believe, think or say about yourself?
3. What negative or false statements have been spoken over (or communicated to) you that you have accepted as true and now say or think about yourself?
4. What Fruit of the Spirit is most difficult for you to keep (Galatians 5:22)? Why?
5. What do you think would bring you joy, peace, relief or freedom?
6. Pray the following prayer. Afterward, sit quietly with Him and write down anything more He reveals.

Father, forgive me for allowing my thoughts to rule over me. I know your Word is Truth and nothing else. I allow you full access to my thoughts. Give me eyes to see how Satan is attacking my thought life and self-talk. Give me grace to expose his plan through my writing. Thank you in advance for your protection, revelation and healing. In Jesus' name, Amen.

STEP 3: EXPOSE YOUR TRIGGERS OR HABITS. What we think and feel eventually pours out into our actions. This is how habits are formed. Specific feelings can become habits because we get used to them. We each have something in our lives that competes with God for our attention. The enemy, who knows our tendencies and triggers, is constantly working to form bad habits and is determined to keep us focused on them. Let these questions open your eyes to your triggers and habits. Write down anything that comes to mind.

1. In hard times, what do you go to instead of God when your heart aches and you want to get away? What do you believe this action will bring?
2. What thoughts, feelings and actions occur when you want to hide or isolate?
3. What areas do you feel stuck, addicted, out of control, empty or broken? Why do you feel this way?
4. What feelings occur after you have indulged in this specific outlet? Why do you feel this way?
5. What may have led to this habit and what triggers it now? Why do you think that?
6. Pray the following prayer. Afterward, sit quietly with him and write down anything more He reveals.

Father, forgive me for allowing life-stealing habits to form. I know they steal from me as well as take my focus off of You and what's true. Jesus, you came to heal my heart and bind up my wounds. I allow you full access to my feelings, thoughts and actions. Give me eyes to see how Satan is attacking me in this area and the grace to expose his plan through my writing. Thank you in advance for your protection, revelation, and healing. In Jesus' name, Amen.

STEP 4: EXPOSE YOUR WOUNDS. Our flesh wants to cover up past experiences that have left us hurting. Negative reactions to situations today come from beliefs and perceived experiences from the past. This is why we believe we have to wear masks. We act like all is well and try to forget, but we cannot heal if we don't expose our wounds to the Light. If left hidden, they will cause further infection. Let these questions open your eyes to past wounds. Write down anything that comes to mind.

1. Pick three defining moments from your past. Describe your experience and the thoughts, feelings and consequences that have resulted.
2. Identify a negative feeling that consumes you at times. This feeling may well be a defense mechanism formed from a past event. When is the first time you remember feeling this way?
3. What theme, pattern or specific area do you see as part of Satan's attack strategy against you?
4. How has your past shaped you (thoughts, feelings and beliefs) and how you view life? How has it shaped your view of God the Father, God the Son and God the Holy Spirit?
5. What has happened in your life that you try to hide, forget or not deal with (i.e. sin, thoughts, events, secrets, etc.)? What is holding you back from giving it to God?
6. Pray the following prayer. Afterward, sit quietly with him and write down anything more He reveals.

Father, forgive me for believing the lie that I am broken beyond repair. You came to heal all of my heart and bind up all of my wounds. I grant you full access to all of my past wounds and beliefs about them that I have bandaged and tried to forget. Please give me eyes to see how Satan is using my wounds to keep me from freedom and abundance. Give me the wisdom and grace to expose his plan through my writing. Remind me to use my tools during this process. Thank you in advance for your protection, revelation and healing. In Jesus' name, Amen.

*Go deeper verses in this chapter: 2 Corinthians 5:20; Philippians 1:6.

11

EXPOSE AND DEMOLISH STRONGHOLDS

The weapons we fight with are not the weapons of the world. On the contrary, they have divine power to demolish strongholds.

— 2 Corinthians 10:4, NIV

Sometime in 2012

Tell others what I'm thinking and going through!?! That is really part of my strategy?

As I allowed this unpopular concept to take hold, a lightness within began to form. The burden of carrying this all-consuming weight alone began to lift. I started to see my "hidden stuff" for what it really was, the enemy's deceptive lies and oppressive attempts to keep me "stuck". Opening up brought me freedom from the secrets and brokenness Satan held over me.

For so long, even the thought of sharing my secrets, sin and pain brought me to a near panic attack. Who knew this very action would begin releasing me from Satan's hold?

Through transparency and vulnerability, we have been given tremendous power to expose the enemy and his plans. The believer's mission is to come alongside God's Heavenly army and fight by:

- Exposing Satan's Lies
- Utilizing our Truth Filter
- Choosing Postures of Surrender
- Applying our Battle Tools

Expose

In Chapter 10, we uncovered common deceptions believers fall prey to:

- *I am supposed to have it all together or at least act like I do.*
- *Since I don't have it all together, I have to hide the areas where I fall short.*
- *God can't use me until I have it all together.*

The enemy's tactics have imprisoned many for so long. Not anymore! He's being exposed. We are coming out of hiding and calling the enemy out. He cannot hold that thing, sin, event, habit or thought over us any longer. We are coming out of darkness and into the light. Out of lies and into the Truth. We are beginning to lay down our broken places at the foot of the cross.

Broken Places

He (Jesus) *heals the brokenhearted and bandages their wounds* (Psalm 147:3).

Our broken places are of the heart. Have you heard that "There's a God shaped hole in all of us?" I'm sure many of you have found this to be true. We all fall short. We are all broken and looking for something to fill that aching place within.

Fortunately, after much searching, some finally see and accept that *It* (the Living Water that heals) and that *Someone* (Jesus) has been right there all along. Unfortunately, many others miss the Truth and continue to look simply at what is seen, only resulting in further emptiness. When we accept Christ as our Savior, He comes into our hearts and occupies that place.

> I've been a Christian for the majority of my life. I also remember experiencing Him fill that space. However, for some reason, even though I was filled, there were times I still "felt" empty. This left me feeling even more confused and ashamed. *If He is in me and fills me, why do I still feel empty right now? What's wrong with me?* I pondered these thoughts for quite some time, and this is what God revealed.

As we've previously discussed, feelings are not Truth. You cannot count on them; however, you must recognize negative feelings as an inner struggle that needs to be addressed. In fact, reoccurring negative feelings and your responses to them most likely originate from a past experience.

So, I put this empty feeling up to the *Triage Challenge*. Asking the following questions helped me identify why I felt empty.

- When was the first time I remember feeling this way? What happened?
- Why did the event make me feel this way?
- Do I remember other times I felt this way?

Once I acknowledged my feelings and why I was feeling them, I ran them through my Truth Filter and determined they were not from God. If it's not from God, Satan is the source. According to our Word Weapon, we are far from empty. Instead, we are full of God who dwells among us, Jesus Christ who lives in us and the Holy Spirit who flows through us.

Picture this: a large bowl full of tiny sealed Tupperware containers. When you pour water into that bowl, the bowl fills up, and the containers float up to the top. The bowl is full of water, but not the containers. They are still empty. Why? Because they are sealed off. Water cannot penetrate and fill up those places because the closed off lids prevent it from doing so.

Believers, we have given Jesus our heart, but not absolute access to it. There are closed off places, or "containers", like hurts, secrets, sins, false beliefs, etc. The Tupperware containers represent our strongholds that have not yet been surrendered, or opened up, to God.

God is a gentleman and although He is pleading for you to fully open yourself to Him, He will not force you to. He is patiently waiting and willing to heal ALL of your broken places *if* you will let Him. Transparency and vulnerability. Only when we are honest with God, ourselves and others will we identify these broken places and open up our "Tupperware lids".

Lesson Learned:
The "empty" feeling I experience from time to time is coming from
a broken place in my heart I'm not inviting the Lord into.

Choose Wisely

A couple of years ago, I fell and broke a bone in my hand. After the injuries were initially accessed, it was obvious I needed a specialist's opinion. The orthopedic specialist told me I had two options:

1. *Wrap the brokenness back up*: I could get a better cast on my hand and allow my body to naturally mend itself as best it could. If I chose this route, my hand would "heal," but I

would never again be able to close it correctly. In fact, my knuckle would actually be gnarled like a street fighter's (yes, those were his actual words). This option was the easiest, lowest cost and less painful choice; but it would bring mediocre results with lifelong consequences.

2. *Undergo surgery:* My hand would heal correctly if I allowed the specialist to surgically mend my brokenness. If so, my hand would be restored back to its intended state of mobility and function. This choice took faith, would be more difficult, costly and painful. However, it would heal completely and increase my quality of life.

Believers, we are at another crossroads and presented with a similar choice. Only we're not talking about just one bone. We are talking about each day of our lives. Are we going to continue self-treating and medicating our broken places that keep us for lack of better words, stuck and living in mediocrity? Or, are we going to allow the Great Surgeon to come in and perform life-giving surgery so we can receive complete healing and a true quality of life?

Sure, it's going to take time and courage. It can be painful, and there will be costs, or sacrifices to be made; but the fullness of your calling is at stake. Surgery of the heart results in a radiance of light, His healing Light shining through and reflecting His glory. This is where we find spiritual abundance!

In order to surrender our broken places, the following must occur:

HONESTY: James 4:10 says, *Humble yourselves before the Lord, and he will exalt you.* We come out of denial or hiding by being honest with:

- *Ourselves* – admitting we aren't perfect and being okay with that. This is, in fact, why Jesus died for us.
- *Others* – admitting our struggles and allowing God to use them to heal us as well as others.
- *God* – admitting we need Him by laying down our pride at the cross and allowing Him full access to this hurt or struggle.

HUMILITY: James 1:5 says, *If any of you lacks wisdom, let him ask God, who gives generously to all without reproach, and it will be given him.* We have to recognize we often don't have all the answers. We need the help of our Counselor who knows all things.

Many times, these strongholds originated from a hurt that has been buried for so long that without His help even identifying the problem or finding the energy to revisit it seems impossible. All we have to do is ask God for help. He promises to show and heal us if we just ask!

SURGERY: Psalm 147:3 says, Jesus *heals the brokenhearted and binds up their wounds.* He is the Great Physician who specializes in healing. We show up for surgery when we surrender our wounds and trust His healing process.

Expose the Strongholds

These battle wounds, or broken places, we have are strongholds. While a stronghold was originally meant for good as a safe place, Satan has twisted the term to mean a wound or accusation deeply rooted, adopted and chosen by us to be held captive to. Most strongholds have become so deeply embedded, we feel we don't have a choice of whether to believe them. *They just are.*

That's a lie! According to 2 Corinthians 10:4, our weapons are *mighty* for pulling down strongholds. It says mighty, not might work. We've been given the fierce, proactive Power to overcome our strongholds. However, in order to pull them down and prevent future ones, we must first understand how they formed.

A stronghold starts with a wrong thought
we identify now as a lie.

This is anything that contradicts what God says. Many of these lies begin in childhood. Unhealthy thinking patterns can form from an event, words spoken over us or simply a random thought that pops in our mind because of something we've done.

My thought, *I should have done better,* over time led to a belief, *my self-worth is based on my performance.* This lie contradicts God Word.

God saved you by his grace when you believed. And you can't take credit for this; it is a gift from God. Salvation is not a reward for the good things we have done, so none of us can boast about it (Ephesians 2:8-9, NLT).

At the time, I didn't know I could choose what to think on, so I accepted the lie as true. Soon the nasty accusation, *I'm not good enough,* was hurled in my direction and I unknowingly welcomed this new thought in. Even though I had accepted Jesus as my Savior, in a way this lie was rejecting His grace covering.

For God made Christ, who never sinned, to be the offering for our sin, so that we could be made right with God through Christ (2 Corinthians 5:21, NLT).

I had accepted the thought, *I'm not good enough,* and begun to agree with Satan, my accuser. Eventually, the *"You're right, I'm failing"* agreement became part of my inner dialogue I would continually repeat. Since we will believe what we hear the most and we cannot get away from ourselves, the more I said, thought or heard something confirming this lie, the more I believed it.

Growing up, I remember not being chosen to be on a team, in a group or the one to date. I remember my mother being frustrated with me in the teen years because I wasn't clean enough, or wouldn't help out enough, or respond the way I should enough. I've looked in the mirror ever since I can remember and felt not thin enough no matter what size I was. I was inadequate, further validating these dangerous agreements that held me captive. The longer I allowed this deception, the further enslaved I became.

In short, my pattern was one of rejection to the point of even rejecting myself. What I failed at tremendously overpowered what I succeeded at, for I only remembered the failures. I received these messages because that is the way I chose to view events in my life, regardless of whether they were true or not.

One day, a new, positive lie entered my gates. *If I keep trying, then I can become good enough* (once again contradicting the verses above). I was blinded. Everything I saw, heard or did was filtered through this new false belief I would continue to fall short of.

What we believe eventually flows out of the heart, often manifesting itself in an outward action or habit. When we get to this point, our minds are so full of hopelessness and condemnation that we try anything to escape, and we believe what we've conjured up is truth.

There's something very wrong with me. I can't stop failing. I couldn't handle these feelings of rejection and failure. They were too much. So, I found outlets (worldly habits) to numb the pain. The outlets became destructive behaviors, which diverted my attention. I started focusing on quitting my new habits, not realizing this was the enemy's ploy to distract and intensify my real wound.

> Our destructive habits are merely a symptom
> of a deeper-rooted problem.

If Satan can get us to focus on discontinuing an outward action instead of correcting the inner turmoil, his strategies of deception and distraction are working.

We can all relate to falling into a vicious cycle at some point. The messages we allow eventually result in strongholds, or "closed off places" where beliefs are strongly defended and suppressed. If we agree, the enemy will continue to build on a stronghold and add layers like an onion. When we take misguided steps to defend ourselves (either through a new lie or worldly outlets), we actually further root the lie(s). Not anymore! It's time we take back our lives!

Demolish the Strongholds

Strongholds were never meant to be a bad thing. In fact, other references to a stronghold in the Bible positively describe it as a fortified place of protection or a fortress. Who was meant to be our Stronghold?

> *The Lord is my rock and my fortress and my deliverer, my God, my rock, in whom I take refuge, my shield, and the horn of my salvation, my stronghold* (Psalm 18:2).

The Bible says God. The deceiver has twisted yet another Truth. Thankfully, we can confidently speak the famous words of Joseph, son of Jacob, *"What Satan intended for my harm, God intended for good."* We can demolish these false strongholds and find solace in our True Rock, Fortress and Redeemer.

> *We destroy arguments and every lofty opinion raised against the knowledge of God, and take every thought captive to obey Christ* (2 Corinthians 10:5).

How do we tear down strongholds? One at a time. We have both the Power and undefeatable Weapon to overcome our deep-rooted false beliefs, by taking every thought to the Lord and making it agree with the Word.

I'm not going to lie. Demolishing wrong thoughts that have become our default thinking is not easy. This is when our boot camp steps up its intensity. Time, intentionality and determination are needed to move forward in implementing your strategy.

In the last *Battle Orders* section, I'm sure things got emotionally raw through self-reflection. Your spiritual muscles should be a little sore. If so, be encouraged; these are growing pains. If you're not a little sore, I challenge you to revisit Triage and go deeper.

If we are willing to "go there" to those places we tend to leave behind or ignore, the miraculous power of the Holy Spirit will show up and bring healing. It takes removing the band-aid we've place on old wounds and targeting them with the one true antibiotic – Jesus, who is the Word.

These wounds, or "containers" have been closed off for long enough. They are bandaged infections that will continue causing further internal damage. No matter how hard we try to push them down and ignore them, they are still there doing great harm. These strongholds need to be treated and demolished for good.

To demolish means to obliterate and remove from existence; target the source and eliminate the false stronghold (lie, belief or mindset) in your mind. Our mind defaults needs to be reset.

Reprogram by habitually casting out wrong thinking and replacing it with Truth thinking. This is part of renewing your mind daily, immersing yourself in prayer and saturating your mind with His Word. Then you can find rest in your true stronghold, the Lord.

Conclusion

You were taught, with regard to your former way of life, to put off your old self, which is being corrupted by its deceitful desires; to be made new in the attitude of your minds; and to put on the new self, created to be like God in true righteousness and holiness (Ephesians 4:22-24, NIV).

As Paul writes his letter to the believers in Ephesus, he reminds them of their ongoing mission, to fight for the life Christ died to give. They had already received Christ. But just as their eyes needed to continually be opened, they continually needed to change into their "spiritual attire." Applying God's Word to our wounds and overall lives is how we remain in our fighting stance.

One of the greatest deceptions is when a believer hears but rationalizes not doing. We have to apply what God says, otherwise there is little hope of it affecting our lives. Truth has to be practiced for it to stick or bring change. The noise of the world constantly fights for our attention.

Let's counterattack by agreeing to surgery.
Just like many surgeries are a matter of life and death,
this tool can be the deciding factor in choosing life.

HEART SURGERY

Chapter 10's Triage Challenge is difficult and complex; but oh, so necessary in uncovering strongholds. It takes time and courage. This exercise is meant to become a life tool because God will continually reveal symptoms and deception when you are ready.

I'm sure walking through this triage the first time brought up feelings of discouragement, fear, anxiety, condemnation or doubt to name a few. I challenge you to reflect on those feelings and ask yourself why. "Why do I feel a certain way?" Also, think back on your life and my stronghold example above. Can you identify a pattern or themed message the enemy has used to keep you stuck and complacent? If the Holy Spirit is bringing anything new to the surface now, go back to your Triage Tool and record your findings.

This process has brought me tremendous healing and continues to be a powerful weapon of defense. However, relief and healing don't fully come until we go under the knife, the double-edged Sword that does not return void.

That brings us to surgery, our next *Battle Orders*. Both prep and surgery take recovery time, they don't need to be rushed. This is the first of many surgeries (depending on how many false strongholds or layers have taken over), so don't be discouraged if there is still more to uncover. As you continue to apply God's word to your wounds, healing will come in His perfect surgical timing.

When showing up for surgery, someone is supposed to remain with you during the procedure. While the Holy Spirit is your Constant Companion and Strength for this process, you are meant to have a battle buddy walk this out with you. During recovery, they encourage, remind and take care of the things you cannot. There will come a point in your orders where you will be challenged to let them read your purging. This is for two reasons:

1. It completes the process of being honest with yourself and others.
2. It gives you an extra set of eyes to help identify those life-stealing lies. Often, we are so close to the problem we can no longer see the deception.

A battle buddy can more easily recognize your lies and speak Truth. They can keep you accountable to continue the process when you want to quit. Implementing this courageous step doubles the stakes and speeds up the healing process.

TRIAGE (REMOVE THE BAND-AID)

+

SURGERY (APPLY THE ANTIBIOTIC)

+

RENEW (SET THE NEW DEFAULT)

=

SUCCESSFUL HEALING AND RECOVERY

TAKE AWAYS

1.

2.

3.

REFLECTION: Find a solitary place and set a timer for 30 seconds. Close your eyes and quiet your mind until the timer goes off.

1. Were you able to quiet your mind? If not, why?
2. Record any thoughts or feelings you experienced.

Many find this exercise difficult. There is a lot of noise fighting for our attention. In order to hear the Holy Spirit's still small voice, the noise must be silenced and removed. If this was difficult for you, be encouraged, the enemy's plans are being exposed! Your weapons are mighty in God for pulling them down.

BATTLE TOOL: Transform (Heart Surgery)

Our winning strategy is a cause and effect process. When we do our part, God will do His. Our job is to open up and expose our brokenness to Jesus. He is both the Light and the Word. Show up for surgery and receive the Great Surgeon's healing.

In Chapter 10's *Battle Orders*, you walked through pre-op, uncovering the deception and pain that has been holding you back. This process takes great courage but reaps glorious reward. Only when we bring our mental garbage to Jesus can we demolish deception and replace it with Truth. You can be free from your strongholds; it's a promise.

Now, we must show up for surgery. We can continue taking a posture of surrender and renewal by immersing ourselves in God's Word and applying His "antibiotic" to our wounds. Then, our Surgeon who has a 100% success rate will work His miracles.

STEP 1: TARGET STRONGHOLDS TO BE DEMOLISHED.

Father, prepare me to walk through heart surgery. As I review my thoughts, please grant me a spirit of wisdom and revelation. Flood the eyes of my heart with light so I may see clearly how the enemy is deceiving me. What pieces of my heart has he taken from me? Where have I given him a foothold? Flood my mind with your Truth. For you Lord are my one and only Stronghold, My Refuge, my Fortress in whom I trust. I surrender my thoughts and trust You to reveal anything in my mind that contradicts Your Word. Thank you in advance for your revelations. In Jesus' name, Amen.

1. Read through your journaling from Chapter 10's Battle Tool, The Triage Challenge. If anything else comes to mind as you read, write it down.
2. Examine each though by asking "Why?" (*Why do I believe that? Or why do I feel that way?*). Write down the results.
3. Filter your writing through Philippians 4:8: *Finally, brothers, whatever is true, whatever is honorable, whatever is just, whatever is pure, whatever is lovely, whatever is commendable, if there is any excellence, if there is anything worthy of praise, think about these things.*
4. What lies, recurring patterns, harmful habits, negative mindsets or false agreements with the enemy can you

identify? (Tip: Reading aloud may help in the identification process.)

5. Mark through anything <u>negative</u> or <u>untrue</u> that you've written with a highlighter to identify your lies.

STEP 2: DEMOLISH ENSLAVED MINDSETS. The enemy uses different tactics to keep our minds from operating the way God intended. Any time the mind is not in a state of peace (even amongst chaos), it is operating via a worldly mentality. It is held captive and seeing things through foggy lenses. This is the enemy's method of distraction, keeping us from who we were meant to be. We were made in the image of God and can have the mind of Christ.

Father, remove any pride and make me open to clearly evaluate the condition of my mind. I know the enemy's plan is to keep me busy and consumed so I cannot hear you. Give me understanding of how he attacks me personally in this area and the wisdom to recognize it. Thank you in advance for revealing Satan's deception and what triggers enslaved mindsets. In Jesus' name I pray. Amen.

1. Look back at your writing, how does the enemy keep you distracted?
2. Which prison, if any, does your mind visit: negativity, anxiousness, doubt, selfishness, fear, pride, criticalness, confusion, busyness, indifference, unbelief, etc.?
3. What enslaved mindsets hold you captive? Give each a name and find at least one Truth (Scripture) that speaks against each. For assistance, search the web topically.
4. Record these in your *Truth Binders*
5. Speak your Truths when tested.

Ex: Enslaved mindset - Worry and Anxiousness

Do not be anxious about anything, but in everything by prayer and supplication with thanksgiving let your requests be made known to God. And the peace of God, which surpasses all understanding, will guard your hearts and your minds in Christ Jesus (Philippians 4:6-7).

STEP 3: DEMOLISH THROUGH HUMILITY AND TRANSPARENCY. To this point, you've walked through the humbling process of being honest with God and yourself. It's now time to take the courageous step to be honest with others. Allow a battle buddy, trusted friend, family member or counselor to review what you've written so far in Triage and steps one or two.

I know this is tough, but I guarantee you will experience a sense of freedom just by allowing others in. When something hidden is brought out into the open, healing occurs! You're picking up your defense weapon of testimony and calling the enemy out. You're beginning to use your story for His glory.

Do not let Satan steal this blessing from you!

Father, give me courage to take this step of obedience as I come out of hiding. I trust you to show me a safe person to share my mental garbage with. I speak against any fear that is holding me back. Protect me from receiving shame or offense as they read through and point out what they see. Give me a humble heart to what they see. May I openly listen and bring it back to you for revelation. Protect my mind from the enemy's tactics to keep me stuck. I thank you in advance for freedom and protection from my strongholds. In Jesus' name I pray. Amen.

1. Step out in faith, remove your mask and watch God work!
2. Give your friend, family member or counselor permission to read through your triage findings.
3. Ask them to highlight any wrong thoughts, attitudes,

mindsets or habits they see that contradict the Word of God. You will be amazed at what others can see just by being outside looking in.

4. Humbly receive their feedback and take it to the Lord.

STEP 4: DEMOLISH LIES AND AGREEMENTS WITH TRUTH. As long as we allow deception a place in our mind, we are inviting the enemy into that wound instead of God. When a lie or agreement is identified and exposed, it must be taken captive (cast out and no longer permitted entry). But there is a second equally important step. Our mind has to be refilled with something and you choose the content. When wrong thoughts and beliefs are cast out, you must choose to replace them with Truth, God's antibiotic. Use your Word Weapon to find Truths that speak directly against lies, agreements, mindsets or beliefs you've uncovered.

1. Take the lie(s) captive. Speak aloud 2 Corinthians 10:4-5 in present tense: *"My weapons have divine power to demolish strongholds. I take (specific thought, sin, lie, etc.) captive and make it obedient to Christ."*

2. Break agreement(s) with the enemy through prayer. What wrong messages have you heard and agreed with? When you agree with the enemy and his lies, you've given him a footing and opened a door. As God's child, you have the power to take back that ground. Pray the following prayer.

Father, forgive me for any unconfessed sin and for making the following agreement "_____" with the enemy. Thank you for bringing it to the light and exposing it for what it is; untrue. In Jesus' name, I break this agreement I have made and ask for your future wisdom, discernment and protection in this area. Thank you for the Truth that sets me free! Amen

3. Replace with Truth. Do a topic or word search of the Bible to find a specific Truth to speak against identified deception.

> Ex: Lie Exposed / Agreement Made – *"I'm not good enough"*
> Root Stronghold: *"Fear that I'm failing, unbelief that Jesus is enough"*

> Replaced Truths to speak aloud when thoughts come in:

> - *There is therefore now no condemnation for those who are in Christ Jesus* Romans 8:1).
> - *Not by might, nor by power, but by my Spirit, says the* LORD *of hosts* (Zechariah 4:6).
> - *There is no fear in love, but perfect love casts out fear. For fear has to do with punishment, and whoever fears has not been perfected in love* (1 John 4:18).

4. Record your Truths in your *Truth Binder.*

5. Continue to speak Truth aloud against deception and negative thinking when tempted.

*Go deeper with verses from this chapter: Ephesians 2:22; Galatians 2:20; 1 Corinthians 3:16; Matthew 7:7; Genesis 50:20; James 1:22.

12

GOD LOVES ME BECAUSE...

GOD loves me, because God LOVES me, because God loves ME...

MARCH 2018

Publishing time was rapidly approaching. The past year of editing *The Believer's Battle Strategy* had been brutal. I was tired. The old thought, *what if it's not good enough,* left me questioning everything. The Spirit prodded me, so I spoke. "God, this is your message and I am just Your messenger."

Assurance washed over me but before I knew it, another arrow appeared. *What if I get in the way and mess up the message?* I spoke in faith, "God, you are sovereign and so much bigger than me."

Doors God opened appeared to start closing and in came confusion and frustration. *God, I thought this was what you wanted? I don't know what I'm doing? Where are you?*

Before I knew it, I was completely overwhelmed at the task before me. So, I went into "shut down" mode and began returning to my old prison feeling of failure. *Why is this happening?*

God whispered, "Christie, go back and read what you've written." I finally listened and took mental inventory. *Triage* revealed fear was my culprit!

Fear was blinding me, decieving me and literally sucking the life out of me... again! God brought 1 John 4:18 to mind, *Perfect love casts out fear.* I started a new *Truth Binder* and recorded the entire verse this time. *Such love has no fear, because perfect love expels all fear.* As I meditated on this verse, I look up different bible translations and this is what I found.

If we are afraid, it is for fear of punishment, and this shows that we have not fully experienced his perfect love (1 John 4:18, NLT).

If we are afraid... we have not fully experienced his perfect love. The words jumped right off the page. I was not only afraid, I was literally paralyzed with fear. Then it hit me, I had closed off my "Tupperware lid" – again!

God loves me. I've heard those three words the majority of my life, yet at times, I still struggle with fully believing them. Fear often becomes my barrier. These lies often follow me like a shadow.

- *I'm not worthy of God's love "yet."*
- *Maybe if I keep trying, then I can be good enough.*

Do you believe God loves you? I mean deep down in your heart and broken places in a way no arrow Satan or the world throws could ever cause doubt? Stop and consider this. If you are thinking, *I already know God loves me;* take caution for it can deceive and steal.

And may you have the power to understand, as all God's people should, how wide, how long, how high, and how deep his love is. May you experience the love of Christ, though it is too great to understand fully. Then you will be made complete with all the fullness of life and power that comes from God (Ephesians 3:18-19, NLT).

Here, Paul reminds us God's love is too great to completely comprehend. Therefore, if we think we already understand God's love, then we don't fully get the overflowing magnitude of it. We know God through the Father. We know God through Christ. We know God through the empowering of the Holy Spirit. But often we are missing the all-encompassing intense nature of God's love because we don't understand it.

God loves you. Period. He wonderfully created you in His perfect image. He makes no mistakes. You are His masterpiece. Why does He love you? Just because. There are no stipulations, conditions or requirements. Simply, *it is finished.* There is nothing you can do to make God love you more. And, there is nothing you can do to make God love you less. He loves you—because!

This Truth is the core of *The Believer's Battle Strategy.* God's Love is your life blood and receiving it is the key to winning the battle. While God's Love is too great for us to fully understand, He desires for us to continually grow, rest and trust in His perfect love. He is an abundant God. He doesn't do or give halfway, the way even the best of love stories play out on screens or in the world. 1 John 4:8 even states that *God IS love*; therefore, He loves to the full until it overflows... and then even more than you can ever ask or imagine!

When considering God's love, I believe most readers fall into one of these general categories:

1. *Those who believe they already know God loves them.* Most have been in church their whole lives. They can sing the song "Jesus loves me this I know, for the Bible tells me so" or quote scripture without hesitation. Not because they truly "get" God's love, but because it's been ingrained in their minds for so long. When God's Word is memorized, it is in our minds; but that doesn't necessarily mean it's reached our hearts. The enemy counts on believers falling into this deception. For this group, God's love is Truth; but it's not *experienced Truth.* It hasn't been received in the heart.

2. *Those who don't personalize God's love for them.* They believe John 3:16 (*For God so loved the world…*) as a blanket statement, but they don't receive His love as an intentional and intimate act meant specifically for them. They don't truly believe God accepts and delights in them alone as an individual and unique creation.

3. *Those who feel unworthy of God's Love.* They believe God can love others, but not them because of what has happened in their past. It's a spinoff of the second category. Whether they've messed up too much or experienced something too horrific, they believe *there is absolutely no way God could possibly love them.* There have been horrendous things that have happened to some. There have also been people who have acted atrociously. This could beg the question, in the world's eyes, can God love that monster because of their actions? Remember, we are not talking about the world's counterfeit concept of love. We are talking about the One who created it and the One who is; God. We have to learn and understand what love really is. 1 John 4:8 says, *Anyone who does not love does not know God, for God is love.* This includes loving yourself.

4. *Those who forget God's love.* They have received revelation and experienced this precious gift, but somewhere along the way, the arrows of pride or complacency have come in and they've unknowingly closed themselves off to the abundance of God's love.

Believers need God's constant flowing love. Otherwise, a circumstance or a lie will creep in, cause doubt and take them back into one of these categories.

What's up with our Lids?

All four groups have something in common. There is a lie or belief averting God's living water from flowing freely. There is a broken place with a Tupperware lid (discussed in the previous chapter) sealed shut and keeping God's life-giving love from fully penetrating their heart. Instead of a continuous flowing spring, there are either dry and empty lands, or a lake that will become complacent or stagnate. When water stagnation occurs, parasites come to feed and decay is the result.

> Picture this: Four clay jars representing believers and the water representing love, our life source we were created to be full of. Each jar is closed and sealed with a lid. They represent the four categories above. Jars 1-3 are completely empty and in need of water. Jar 4 does contain water; however, it's no longer flowing and the water will become stagnant if it hasn't already. All four jars have closed themselves off from receiving water, God's continuous Love.

Regardless of the category that most describes you, let's all remove our lids and seek residency in a fifth group; *clay jars that remain open to believing and receiving all of God's love.*

This requires humility and determination. May I suggest revisiting the Triage Challenge (in Chapter 10) with a focus of God's love for you. I believe most of our broken places stem from either unbelief or misunderstandings about God's Love.

> *And I am convinced that nothing can ever separate us from God's love. Neither death nor life, neither angels nor demons, neither our fears for today nor our worries about tomorrow—not even the powers of hell can separate us from God's love* (Romans 8:38-39, NLT).

> God loves you. There is nothing or no one who can
> keep you from His love. However, there is *someone*
> who can keep you from *experiencing* His love.
> It's not the enemy, it's yourself.

Remember, we are the doorkeepers of our mind and heart. God is a gentleman and will not force Himself on you. This includes His love.

God's love is absolute, constantly flowing and never changing, but if we remain closed off by lies, we will not experience it.

Unfortunately, this is the true human state for the majority, maybe even the 8 out of 10 believers spoken of in Chapter 4. Not accepting and receiving God's love has enslaved most from this amazing free gift for far too long. Satan is hell-bent on warping our view of real Love and filling our lives with moments of rejection to confirm our unworthiness. He will use every tactic he can to keep us from getting this foundational Truth.

> Satan knows if you truly understand love,
> you will know God, you will know who God is,
> and therefore you will know who you truly are.

God loves me *because*. Our finite minds can't grasp this concept. Why and how could God love something so broken? We think there has to be something more to it. For this reason, we need evidence because we are faced daily with the world's contradiction of love.

Let's correct this universal lie and amend these misperceptions and assumptions. God's Word holds the answer and the ammunition to counter attack what the enemy and this world have told us.

Your God Picture

Close your eyes and get a mental picture of God. Which of the following best describes your experience? Do you see God as distant and impersonal, or maybe like my son once said 'really big and kind of scary'? Do you see him as a micro-managing taskmaster always watching and waiting for you to mess up?

Or is God personal and intimate, your daddy in heaven who loves you so much He can't take His eyes off of you? This is Truth. God desires an authentic relationship with you. He wants to bless and fill you with the abundance of Christ.

Often, the image or feeling we get when attempting to picture our Heavenly Father directly correlates with the way we view our earthly father. I'm sure you can imagine the wide spectrum of pictures and feelings God the Father brings to minds. Many had a decent childhood resulting in positive pictures, while many others have experienced indifference, abuse or even abandonment.

The good news is none of these pictures are true. We all have the same Heavenly Father, and He never changes. Regardless of your father picture, this belief is coming from the world and your circumstances. Our God picture, which ultimately is love, must align with the Word and not the world. Knowing God and His love comes with filling your mind with Truth. We do this by meditating on, accepting His love and allowing His Spirit to reveal more.

The world says love is a feeling, but the Word says love is a choice!

"For you are a people holy to the Lord your God. The Lord your God has chosen you to be a people for his treasured possession, out of all the peoples who are on the face of the earth. It was not because you were more in number than any other people that the Lord set his love on you and chose you, (Deuteronomy 7:6-7a).

CHOSEN. I've debated with friends on this one and even seen one walk away from a marriage because he no longer "felt" love towards his spouse. Oh, has the enemy twisted this one.

The world says:

- *When you feel love for someone marry them or surround yourself with them.*
- *When you no longer feel love for someone, get rid of them and replace them with someone who makes you feel loved.*

If this is your reasoning on love, you will eventually end up alone. That love you feel for that someone will be tested because that someone will one day let you down. And if you haven't already, you will also let a loved one down. No one is perfect, except God who is love. Let's look to Him for Truth in this term the world has overused and perverted.

I'm sure God experiences a variety of emotions when it comes to us, and I'm sure it's not always this warm, gooey love feeling the world has conjured up. The Truth is God chose you to love. It's a promise. According to John 17:6, you're the Father's special treasure and gift to Jesus. Read that again. This Truth will never change because love is not a feeling, it's a choice.

> I have loved you, my people, with an everlasting love (Jeremiah 31:3a, NLT).

EVERLASTING. Eternal. Never-ending. God's love was sealed when Christ shed His blood for you. In fact, God's love was sealed even in the beginning when God said, *Let there be light*, for this beautiful mystery was His plan all along. Love – real love – is unchanging; therefore, it cannot be based on feelings.

God chose to love you even before you were created. This means it has nothing to do with what you can do or have done. He chose to send His Son to die in your place so you could spend eternity with Him. Of course, God didn't *feel* like sacrificing His Son and watching Him experience such an excruciating death.

Lesson Learned:
God allowed His love sacrifice ... because!

The world says love is conditional, but the Word says love is unconditional.

With unfailing love I have drawn you to myself (Jeremiah 31:3b, NLT).

UNFAILING. Constant. Steady. Love is unconditional; loving someone regardless of what they've done in the past, what they are currently doing or what they may do in the future. We are the bride of Christ; therefore, we are in a spiritual marriage. Marriage the way it was meant to be, bound and committed for life no matter what.

Conversely, the world sees marriage as an agreement, a give and take contract formed with stipulations that can become null and void if the deal is broken. While we often find ourselves living narcissistically with irreconcilable differences or committing adulteries of the heart, our Spiritual Spouse does not waver in His commitment towards us. He remains steady and constant. There is *nothing* we can do to "separate" this marriage. We need to pray for God to open up our eyes to true love; Him.

I'm too broken, flawed or sinful. How could God possibly love me?

If you hear this lie, receive the Truth. God is saying:

I love you anyway. I no longer see what you've done. I care what you've been through though, for I was right beside you the whole time. I sent my Son to die for all of your past, present, and future sins and hurts. You are covered by the shed blood of Jesus Christ and clothed in His righteousness. This was finished before you even breathed your first breath. When I look at you, I see Jesus... clean, pure, sanctified, and complete. Will you let Me love you?

Lesson Learned:
God loves you unconditionally ... because!

The world says love is earned, but the Word says love is freely given.

And since it is through God's kindness, then it is not by their good works. For in that case, God's grace would not be what it really is--free and undeserved (Romans 11:6, NLT).

FREE AND IMPARTED. At no cost. In the world's eyes, who is most adored? It's the wealthy, successful, beautiful and (fill in the blank). I find myself falling back into this trap occasionally.

My worth and acceptance are based on performance or becoming better at something. When I believe this, I'm being deceived. While I don't believe I'm doing anything to earn God's love, I still believe I'm doing things to be worthy of this love He's chosen to give me.

We must stop and take these thoughts captive. Our Truth Filter shows us there is no difference between these two thoughts. If we have to be worthy of God's love, then Christ did not have to die. He shed his blood to completely cover us and freely give us His righteousness. All we have to do is accept it. This free gift is not based on anything we have or ever can do.

I *don't deserve God's love.*
I'm not good enough. I'm too flawed to love.
I have to change some things about me before He can love me.

If you hear any of these lies, receive the Truth. Again (and someone needs to hear this), God is saying:

I love you anyway. I no longer see what you've done. I care what you've been through though, for I was right beside you the whole time. I sent my Son to die for all of your past, present, future mistakes and shortcomings. You are covered by the shed blood of Jesus Christ and clothed in His righteousness. This was finished before you even breathed your first breath. When I look at you, I see Jesus… perfect, pure, sanctified and complete. Will you let Me love you?

Lesson Learned:
God freely gave His gift of love … because!

How do we let God Love us?

As we come to more fully understand God's love, there is a prerequisite to experiencing His love. We have to choose to let Him love us. We must accept His free gift. This very moment, God has His "water pitcher" set in place, ready to pour out and saturate His clay jars as soon as our lids are opened to receive. He's waiting for you to block out the world instead of His love. Stop striving for what is already yours. Instead, focus solely on Him and receive His love. This is how we truly experience *the love of Christ which surpasses knowledge and the fullness of God.*

I've been a believer for about 30 years. However, it wasn't until watching a Joyce Meyer teaching 11 years ago that I realized I had never sat in quiet and truly meditated on God's love for me. Instead I had been drowning in condemnation. It was when I started meditating (thinking, speaking and focusing) on His love and His Word instead of just reading it that my eyes began to open and chains began to break. I began to experience His love for the first time.

Oxford English Dictionary defines meditate as to think deeply or focus one's mind for a period of time, in silence, or with the aid of chanting, for religious or spiritual purposes or as a method of relaxation.

When I read this, I feel caution because it makes me think of New Age practices. But this is just another way the enemy has twisted Truth. As a matter of fact, meditation originated in the Bible, and it is a good thing. Turning God's love and His promises over and over in our minds is life-giving and transforming. In fact, Jesus often went to a solitary place to just be with His Father.

It is when we meditate on God's Word day and night that it heals us and sets us free. It is in meditating that the Lord gives us understanding; when Truth becomes more than just head knowledge and we experience heartfelt intimacy with the Almighty.

Synonyms for meditate include "intercede" and "reconcile." Jesus both intercedes and reconciles us back to the Father. Please note, if Jesus is not the center of your meditation, the enemy can use this practice for his purposes.

> And I pray that you, being rooted and established in love, may have power, together with all the Lord's holy people, to grasp how wide and long and high and deep is the love of Christ, and to know this love that surpasses knowledge —that you may be filled to the measure of all the fullness of God (Ephesians 3:17b-19, NIV).

God has to be given full access to grow His love roots deep. It is then that we are made strong. Let Him pour out His love over you and fill you to the full. If you remain open and steadfast to experiencing His love anew, this continual spring will overflow into your life and relationships.

Lesson Learned:
I must meditate on God's love in order to receive it.

Conclusion

Love endures with patience and serenity, love is kind and thoughtful, and is not jealous or envious; love does not brag and is not proud or arrogant. It is not rude; it is not self-seeking, it is not provoked [nor overly sensitive and easily angered]; it does not take into account a wrong endured. It does not rejoice at injustice, but rejoices with the truth [when right and truth prevail]. Love bears all things [regardless of what comes], believes all things [looking for the best in each one], hopes all things [remaining steadfast during difficult times], endures all things [without weakening] (1 Corinthians 13:4-7, AMP).

Love never fails. We often put our focus on expressing 1 Corinthians 13 towards others. But stop, read it again and meditate on the fact that this is *first* God's expression towards you.

UNCONDITIONAL. UNFAILING. EVERLASTING!

BATTLE ORDERS
Ch 12 - God Loves Me Because

TAKE AWAYS

1.

2.

3.

REFLECTION:

1. Close your eyes and picture God. Record what you see and feel. Evaluate how it lines up with Truth?
2. Which of the four categories from the beginning of this chapter do you fall into? Explain.
3. What lie do you hear that keeps your "lid" closed off from receiving all of God's love?
4. *God Loves Me.* What, if any, *"but"* and *"if"* conditions have you added to this absolute?

Ex: God loves me, BUT I'm not good enough yet. I need to earn that love first. Or God will love me if/when I do a, b and c.

Walk back through Heart Surgery,
open your "lid" and let the Truth set you free.

BATTLE TOOL: Experience (God Loves Me Meditation)

Find a solitary place. Ask the Lord to quiet your mind and walk through the following steps. (Once this meditation is a habit, you will be able to implement it anywhere).

1. Speak aloud "God Loves Me" when you feel your mind reach a calm state.
2. Mediate on this phrase. What does it mean to you? Receive it.
3. Repeat step two, emphasizing and focusing on a different word each time. "GOD loves me. God LOVES me. God loves ME."
4. Sit with God until you start to experience His love.
5. Practice this tool not once, not twice, but daily for a week and watch what the Lord reveals! Switch it up. Stand in front of a mirror and speak it. Ask the Lord to show you what you mean to Him and how He see you. Speak different verses about God's love. Tweak as He leads.
6. Make this hymn one of your first defenses in the midst of an attack. Each time you feel a spiritual assault, execute the *God Loves Me* Battle Tool.

*Go deeper verses in this chapter: Ephesians 1:9; Galatians 2:21; 1 Corinthians 5:21; 2 Corinthians 4:7; Psalm 1:1-3; John 8:32; Proverbs 4:20-22.

13

IT'S WHO I AM

You're a good, good father. It's who you are ... and I'm loved by You. It's who I am...

— CHRIS TOMLIN

WHO ARE YOU?

When asked this question, I often find myself rambling off a list of achievements, status, strengths or who I know just to try and prove my worth: *Mother to three, friend of many, wife to George, sister to a pastor, ministry leader, writer, American, high school homecoming queen, etc.*

I then find my mind mentally listing all the things "wrong" with me: *overweight, freckly, frizzy headed, sugar addict, at risk for cancer, inconsistent, rejected, lazy, stupid, depressed, disorganized, scattered, not enough, etc.*

Who are you?

We all have our man-made identity list. These lists can go on and on and unfortunately, aside from what we do, the negative list is the easiest to come up with. If I told you I am none of these things, nor are you your list, would you believe me?

Believers, we are being deceived by the ways of the world.

- Physical characteristics do not define us.
- Who we know doesn't define us.
- What we do doesn't define us.

These things are not who we are. This is *identity theft* and it has the enemy written all over it.

The apostle John was one of the 12 disciples and one of the exclusive New Testament writers. He was asked by Jesus to look after His mother following the Savior's death. He was also the only disciple who wasn't martyred, and it wasn't from any lack of persecution. In fact, John was immersed in boiling oil, yet that didn't take his life.

Finally, as a last resort, he was exiled to the Island of Patmos where he wrote the book of Revelation and lived out his final days. As I introduce him into this chapter, John seems like a pretty important guy. However, this is not who he is.

John is the *one whom Jesus loved.* In the gospel of John, he wrote this about himself not once but three times. I used to laugh at the arrogance of this, but if you think about it, John most definitely was one of the few believers who truly "got" it. He knew who he was. God loved John, uniquely and extravagantly. John boasted in this Truth and confidently proclaimed it!

God loves you uniquely and extravagantly. What if we all stepped out and embraced John's kind of faith in the Father's love? What if the next time someone asks you about yourself, you told them you are the one whom Jesus loves? My friends, that's exactly who we are. Let's forget our man-made identity lists and focus instead on God's!

I know some readers are feeling skeptical right now, thinking: John was greater because He was one of Jesus' inner circle.

There is neither Jew nor Greek, there is neither slave nor free, there is no male and female, for you are all one in Christ Jesus (Galatians 3:28).

We've just taken that lie captive and replaced it with Truth.

The Ones whom Jesus Loved

We are created uniquely and equally in God's image. We are also a gift to Jesus from His Father (John 17:6). Let that sink it. The next time someone asks us who we are, let's confidently proclaim our spiritual inheritance. "I am a beloved child of God!" Reject that old, phony list of yours and don't go another day being deceived. Embrace your true identity!

When people used to ask me about myself, my first reply was, I'm just a mom. While this is such an important and life-changing calling, I still felt like I was supposed to be doing more to prove my worth. Before that, I would say my accomplishments in high school, what degree I was studying for or what job I had at the time.

About 11 years ago, God revealed Himself to me in a new way. Since then, He's planted in me a passion for ministry, writing and teaching. Now, when I'm asked, "Ministry Leader" is the first thing I say, as I continue to try and convince others of my worthiness. This one is trickier because it's about Him, however, my focus is on what I can do for God. It's not who I am.

I dug even deeper and asked myself what defines me, what I focus on most and what determines my days as successes or failures. Guess what I uncovered? It's what the scale says or how I feel about my physical size on a given day. Yep, that's the trivial, worldly hang-up I have allowed to define me, and to steal, kill and destroy.

In the past I have viewed the scale as the indicator of my worth. It's my high place where I either praise myself or tear myself down depending on numeric results. A number I would sear into my brain each morning that would bring either pride or condemnation for the day. Even now, I still have to remind myself I am not what I do, nor what I weigh.

The answers to my identity came with journaling and introspection. In this chapter's *Battle Orders,* I challenge you to do the same, for we all fall into the trap of finding our worth and identity in something other than God. Once deception is uncovered, it's time to cast out the lies and make your thoughts obey the Word.

Lesson Learned:
In order to understand who you are, you must truly know who God is.

God is Love

I keep asking that the God of our Lord Jesus Christ, the glorious Father, may give you the Spirit of wisdom and revelation, so that you may know him better (Ephesians 1:17, NIV).

In the previous chapter, we learned this, and He poured that love out onto us, His children, by sending His Son, Jesus, to die in our place. Have you executed the *God Loves Me* Battle Tool, meditating on and experiencing His all-encompassing love? If not, stop right now and keep walking through your *Battle Orders* from Chapter 12.

Some of us have large barriers (lies we believe and certain mindsets) keeping us from experiencing God's love. If this is you, don't stop pursuing. Identify your lies and take them to the Great Surgeon. Definitely don't stop meditating on Truth. Thank God in advance for breaking down those barriers and revealing His love to you.

God is 3 in 1

I pray that the eyes of your heart may be enlightened (Ephesians 1:18, NIV).

There are things about God we will not fully understand this side of heaven. One is the Holy Trinity. God is one God, yet three persons: God the Father, God the Son and God the Holy Spirit. The best picture and understanding I've received this far is from a children's book by Joanne Markhausen called *Three in One: A Picture of God.*

The author compares the concept of God to an apple. As an apple has three parts (core, skin and flesh), God is three persons (Father, Son and Holy Spirit). Each part of the apple has a different role and purpose, yet they are all one apple. Similarly, each Person of the Trinity has a different role and purpose, yet they are all one God. While we can't limit the concept of God to this picture, it's a start to understanding who He is.

God the Father is Good

Give thanks to the LORD, *for he is good, for his steadfast love endures forever* (Psalm 136:1).

Our Creator and Sustainer. Our Provider and Protector. The Beginning and End of all things. The Father dwells among believers and is good *all* the time. Given the state of the world today, many question this. If God is good, why do bad things happen to good people? It's a valid question that's hard to answer. A question we need our spiritual eyes for to see and understand. But first, here's a question I must ask. If Jesus is our standard, who among us is good anyway?

Romans 3:23 says, *for all have sinned and fall short of the glory of God;* therefore, none of us are good. Since God is love, there's no pressure in any way on any of us to be or do something. Out of His complete love, we are free to choose Him or to choose another way.

Unfortunately, many permanently choose another way. Even believers temporarily choose things over Him such as material goods, self, other people, etc. While this does not change believers' eternal state, it does affect the circumstances around them. I am preaching to myself here.

It's not God who causes bad things, it's our flesh combined with the enemy's manipulative tactics. While God gives man free will and our choices affect others, we can always be assured of this, He remains all powerful. Only what He allows will happen; and when it does, He promises to use even the bad for our good.

Our time on earth is but a blip on our true lifeline. We must keep a Kingdom perspective and focus on eternal consequences instead of short-term ones. Our lives are meant to be living testimonies to the dying world, and those testimonies often come out of our "bad things." If you allow Him to, God will use your pain for His good purposes!

God the Father is I AM

God said to Moses, "I AM WHO I AM..." Exodus 3:14 (NIV)

All knowing. All powerful. Always present. Our Heavenly Father who *decided in advance to adopt us into his own family by bringing us to himself through Jesus Christ. This is what He wanted to do, and it gave Him great pleasure* (Ephesians 1:5, NLT).

He loves you because. He chose you because. Since you are a beloved child of God, *you* are *a* chosen *people, a* royal *priesthood, a* holy *nation, God's* special possession, *that you may declare the praises of him who called you out of darkness into his wonderful light* (1 Peter 2:9, emphasis mine).

God the Son is also I AM

... that you may know the hope to which he has called you, the riches of his glorious inheritance in his holy people (Ephesians 1:18b, NIV).

Jesus Christ. Our Savior and Redeemer. The Lion and the Lamb. The Prince of Peace called to die so you could live. In the gospel of John, Jesus uses "I am" statements to illustrate to the world Who He really is:

I am the Bread of life (John 6:35, 48).
I am the Light of the world (John 8:12, 9:5).
Before Abraham was, I am (John 8:58).
I am the door (John 10:9).
I am the good shepherd (John 10:11).
I am the resurrection and the life (John 11:25).
I am the way, the truth and the life (John 14:6).
I am the true vine (John 15:1).

All of Jesus' "I am" statements point to Him as God and the only way to life and abundance. Christ is God the Son. At creation, He was there and a willing participant of God the Father's perfect plan. He came to earth to defeat physical and spiritual death. He came to be our representative and substitute. He came to take the consequence for our violations of the law. He became our ultimate sacrifice, which fully cleanses us. He is life. This is our inheritance simply by coming to Him with a repentant heart.

I have been crucified with Christ. It is no longer I who live, but Christ who lives in me (Galatians 2:20a).

Did you hear that? When we take our place in His death (throw off our old, sinful nature and crucify the flesh), we are raised up to a new life in Him. Christ lives *in* you. Stop and truly receive this. Aside from *God Loves you*, it's the second most important Truth for you to fully embrace. His blood sacrifice covers you completely; therefore, you are now *in* Him.

This means you are all the things He says about you! Remember that old discarded list about your identity? Here's your new one straight from God.

Who Am I?

I AM IN CHRIST; THEREFORE I AM ...

Beloved. His bride, child, clothed, complete, holy and without blame, redeemed, forgiven, baptized, a joint heir, a holy temple, adopted, royalty, sanctified, not in need, more than a conqueror, more than an overcomer, set free from the law, a powerful vessel, fearfully and wonderfully made, a masterpiece, protected, God's worker, sealed, given the Holy Spirit as the source of our strength...

Read this mind-blowing list to yourself again. Now, read it out loud. Don't rush through it. Try saying it to yourself in front of a mirror. Search the scriptures and see the proof for yourself. This is your true identity in Christ, and guess what? It's only the beginning! Receive your God-given identity. Stop, marinate and digest this "manna" daily.

Lesson Learned:
Remembering who and Whose you are is how to keep a Kingdom perspective.

In Christ, I am Made Right

For our sake he made him (Jesus) to be sin who knew no sin, so that in him we might become the righteousness of God (2 Corinthians 5:21).

Jesus' blood shed for you has fully cleansed your sin and covered your shortcomings. You are completely forgiven – past, present and future. Our amazing God doesn't stop there. When Jesus rose from the grave, He also granted you *His* righteousness. It is not a righteousness you have to work for. If that were so, why would Christ have to die?

You are given Christ's righteousness. This means you no longer have to work to be or prove worth or right standing. You already are made worthy and right because of His righteousness alone. When God the Father looks at you, He sees His son, Jesus. Wow!

In Christ, I am a New Creation

Therefore, if anyone is in Christ, he is a new creation. The old has passed away; behold, the new has come (2 Corinthians 5:17).

Since we've been crucified with Christ, we've been raised to a new life like He was. This doesn't say, we are improved or will become better when we try harder. It says the old is already gone. If you are in Christ, you are brand spanking new! This newness is Christ living in you. This is your new identity! Christ and your Word Weapon include an overwhelming description for you and they are all the evidence you need!

In Christ, I am Complete

So you also are complete through your union with Christ, who is the head over every ruler and authority (Colossians 2:10, NLT).

Complete means full and not lacking. You are enough, and Christ is enough for you! Is anyone hearing this and thinking, *If I am made*

right, complete and new; then how come I still sin and struggle with some of
the same things I did before Christ?

I still hear that one and have to repeat the gospel often to protect myself from this lie. The Truth is, while I am changing and becoming more like Him each day, the process isn't as fast as I would like for it to be.

Unfortunately, as long as we are alive in this world, we will still sin and struggle. However, we are no longer a slave to it. When we came to Christ, our old nature was removed; and through faith, we were made right, complete and new. This is Truth, even when we don't *feel* or *look* like it yet on the outside.

> Picture this: An onion has to be plucked from the ground to be used. Once plucked, it has a new life and will be fulfilling its purpose. When you peel it, there are many layers and often this peeling process will bring tears to your eyes. As the layers are peeled they are separate, or no longer part of the onion core. While you can place the onion layers back on the onion for a time, they are still cut off and no longer attached.

We are like that onion, with layers to be peeled. Those layers are parts of our old self still connected to the world. Once we are chosen, pulled up from out of the world and born again; these layers are cut off and begin to die. As we grow closer to Christ, He reveals to us more and more of these layers to lay aside. These layers are already dead because we are now alive in Christ (out of the world and in His hands); however, they are still present to trip us up when we allow it.

The enemy wants you to believe your old nature is still a part of you, and when you agree with him on this, you're picking those layers up and stacking them back on. They may feel like you, but they are not you. They are merely a part of your past before Christ.

Lesson Learned:
Regardless of my feelings, I will proclaim the Truth: "I am IN Christ;
therefore, I am enough, made right and complete. A new creation!"

God the Holy Spirit is Infinite Power

I also pray that you will understand the incredible greatness of God's power
for us who believe him (Ephesians 1:19, NLT).

Our Constant Companion, Guide, Counselor, Advocate and Strength. God's great Power. As adopted children, we have received an inheritance beyond measure. The Holy Spirit is our deposit guarantee (our foretaste and evidence) of what's to come. He (yes, He's a person) was placed into each believer at the moment of adoption (salvation).

If you call on Jesus as your Lord, you have the Holy Spirit living inside of you this very moment! It took some time for me to comprehend this. In fact, I'm still learning the magnitude of it. The Holy Spirit is a free gift to all believers. When we allow Him, He provides:

- Guidance for our mission.
- Moment by moment counsel, instruction and conviction.
- Intercession on our behalf.
- Sufficient Strength in our weakness.

The more you come to know Him, the more of His power you will experience.

Ephesians 1:20 (NLT) goes on to say, *This is the same mighty power that raised Christ from the dead and seated him in the place of honor at God's right hand in the heavenly realms.*

He is the same power that hovered over the earth in the beginning.

He is the same power that came upon called individuals who prophesied and performed miracles in the Old Testament. He is the same power that came down from heaven and rested on Jesus at His baptism. And, He is the same power seen through Christ's crucifixion, resurrection and ascension.

The same power, the Holy Spirit, lives inside of you! Just like we have the free will to choose to experience God's love, we also have the choice to draw on the Holy Spirit's power. The sin and struggles we face are no match for us as new creations in Christ drawing upon the power of the Holy Spirit. This Mighty Current flowing through us is unstoppable. Therefore, we can overcome, *because greater is He who is in us, than he who is in the world.*

Lesson Learned:
We can have as much of the Holy Spirit as we want
IF we pursue the relationship.

Conclusion

We all have a standard of what we believe we are supposed to be as well as where we fall short. Unfortunately, the world constantly screams its opinion, causing us to become distracted with comparison and unrealistic expectations that constantly kill, steal and destroy. Who are you allowing to define you, the world or Jesus?

Take time to pause and reflect back on God's Truth in this chapter. Many may've already heard or know these verses. However, be honest and ask yourself if these promises have reached your heart.

Are God's promises for you head knowledge
(memorized and familiar) or heart knowledge (received)?

BATTLE ORDERS
Ch 13 - It's Who I Am

TAKE AWAYS

1.

2.

3.

REFLECTION:

1. Who are you? List everything that comes to mind. Then answer the following questions to complete your list:

- What defines you? (i.e. appearance, education, who you know, what you do, another person, etc.)
- Who or what determines your days as successes or failures?
- What or who determines your worth?
- What do you focus on or give your time to the most?
- What do you want to be like? Who do you compare yourself to? Why?
- What negative thoughts about yourself consume your mind?

2. Look at your man-made list formed from above and see it for what it really is, a contradiction of Truth. Go to the Bible and your Truth

Binder. Correct your list by crossing out what you or the world says, and replacing it with what God says.

Ex: *I am ugly. I am a mother. I am poor.*

Truth:

- *I am fearfully and wonderfully made* (Psalm 139:14.)
- *I am a child of God* (Galatians 3:26).
- *I am royalty* (1 Peter 2:9).

BATTLE TOOL: Remember (Identity Object)

To have identity transformation, we need a constant reminder of who we are.

1. Review the chapter and God's Word to find scriptures that speak of who you are. (For a list of I Am Declarations, visit believersbattlestrategy.com.)
2. Choose "Identity" scriptures that you struggle believing or receiving. Always include I am Beloved in your list.
3. Declare these scriptures over yourself every day for one week. *Ex: There is no condemnation for me, for I am in Christ* (Romans 8:1).
4. Take this statement, "I am (what God says I am) IN Christ," and complete it with your verse. *Ex: I am forgiven in Christ.*
5. Find a physical object to place on your wrist (i.e. bracelet, string, marker, etc.) to remind you who you are. Every time you see it, feel it or remember it's there; speak your identity Truths.

*Go deeper verses from this chapter: Isaiah 55:9; Romans 8:28; 1 John 4:4.

14

RECLAIM AUTHORITY

Behold, I have given you authority to tread on serpents and scorpions, and over all the power of the enemy, and nothing shall hurt you.

— Luke 10:19

2015 Charleston, SC

Waves of nausea continued to flood over me. I didn't have a weak stomach and I knew I wasn't pregnant. Days turned into weeks and the nausea persisted. I began spending most of my time with the covers over my head, trying to get away from the physical discomfort. *What's wrong with me?*

During response time at church, I'd had enough. I went to receive prayer from elders of the church. As I was telling them what I was going through, they sensed more than just a physical issue. They began to pray against a spiritual resistance with a boldness I had never experienced.

As soon as they prayed against anxiety, I became so consumed with nausea, I could barely stand. They then asked me to repeat a prayer aloud. In the mighty name of Jesus, I boldly repeated and prayed against the enemy and his work warring against me in that moment.

I kid you not, from that point on my nausea was gone. I left church that day amazed, and once again reminded just how real this spiritual battle is. A few weeks later, there were times where I felt the nausea resurface. Each time, I exercised my power and authority against it in prayer, and each time it ceased.

THE SPIRITUAL BATTLE IS REAL! Why is this so hard to believe? Why do we allow ourselves to forget? In the Bible there are examples after examples of the attack, how it affects us and how to fight back.

Jesus is our Supreme Example to follow. Not only did He come to live IN us, He also came to teach and model FOR us on how to live. Yes, Christ is *in* us; but we must do our part and allow Christ to live *through* us. We must decrease and learn from Him as He increases.

The Example

And when Jesus was baptized, immediately he went up from the water, and behold, the heavens were opened to him, and he saw the Spirit of God descending like a dove and coming to rest on him; and behold, a voice from heaven said, "This is my beloved Son, with whom I am well pleased" (Matthew 3:16-17).

At the beginning of Jesus' ministry, John the Baptist had the opportunity to baptize and reveal who Jesus really was. This was God's Beloved Son. Our Perfect Example. This is who Jesus is. After this incredible introduction, Jesus was led by the Spirit into the wilderness to be tempted.

Did you catch that? The Spirit led Jesus there to be tempted, not to tempt. It then says Jesus fasted and prayed for forty days and nights, becoming very weak and hungry. Since God is all knowing, the encounter with the enemy was no sneak attack. It was part of God's plan. Similar to Job, God granted Satan permission to attack, or test Jesus even at His weakest.

Our battles are meant to refine and strengthen us for our callings whether they are intentioned or just allowed by God. I believe Jesus' test was given not only to prepare Him for His ministry, but more importantly, to teach us how to respond when under attack. Jesus was fully man, fully God; therefore, He understands what we face when tempted by Satan and the world each day. In Luke 4:1-13, Jesus demonstrates for us how to stand our ground.

> *The devil said to him, "If you are the Son of God, command this stone to become bread"* (Luke 4:3, emphasis mine).

I don't know about you, but only one day without food is enough to make me ravenous and not care about anything else. Jesus had fasted for 40 days. The level of temptation present for Him had to be overwhelming. This assault is the obvious one, but notice there is also an underlying one. Satan attacks Jesus' identity. He often does the same to us. Consider the following:

- *If you are a child of God, then why would _____ be happening?*
- *If you were really a Christian, then why would God treat you this way?*
- *If you were really In Christ, then why can't you _____?*
- *If God really loved you, then why did He allow _____?*

Do you ever hear or think similar if/then accusations? These are the enemy's assaults on your identity. Now, watch what Jesus does.

> *And Jesus answered him, "It is written, 'Man shall not live by bread alone'"* (Luke 4:4, emphasis mine).

How did Jesus respond? He already knew who He was, so He quoted scripture, Deuteronomy 8:3, right back at Satan with confidence. Here, Jesus gives us a practical example of how to use our double-edged Sword.

STRIKE ONE, FIERY DART AVERTED!

And the devil took him up and showed him all the kingdoms of the world in a moment of time, and said to him, "To you I will give all this authority and their glory, for it has been delivered to me, and I give it to whom I will. If you, then, will worship me, it will all be yours" (Luke 4:5-7).

Satan switched tactics and appealed to man's desire to be worshiped and have worldly power and material goods.

*Then Jesus said to him, "*Be gone, Satan!* For it is written, "'You shall worship the Lord your God and him only shall you serve'"* (Matthew 4:10, emphasis mine).

Notice I used Matthew's version of this part in Jesus' story. His perspective adds another technique to model. With Satan's second assault, Jesus boldly commanded Satan to leave and then quoted more scripture (Deuteronomy 6:13). Even though at this point, it looked and sounded as if Satan had the authority, Jesus knew the Truth and used it against him.

STRIKE TWO, FIERY DART AVERTED!

And he took him to Jerusalem and set him on the pinnacle of the temple and said to him, "If you are the Son of God, throw yourself down from here, for it is written, "'He will command his angels concerning you, to guard you,' and "'On their hands they will bear you up, lest you strike your foot against a stone'" (Luke 4:9-11).

First, Satan's attacks are getting stronger and sneakier. In this instance, Satan even quoted scripture (Psalm 91:11) in his deception. But Jesus knew His Father's Word well enough to know the deceiver was taking it out of context. There are no contradictions in God's Word. This is a warning we cannot skip over. Satan knows the Word, unfortunately maybe even better than us; therefore, he knows how to twist it. We must know God's Word in its context so we will not be deceived.

Second, Satan attacked Jesus' identity again with an accusation. *If you are who you are, then prove it!* If Satan will spend the majority of his time attacking Jesus' identity, then how many more twisted lies will he throw us about who we are as children of God? Since we need to be reminded of our identity often, we must form lifelong habits of speaking what God says about us to keep our Breastplates (of Righteousness) in place.

Jesus responded, "The Scriptures also say, 'You must not test the LORD your God' (Luke 4:12).

Jesus recognized the deception coming at Him and corrected the enemy with Deuteronomy 6:16 in context. He did not waiver in Who He was. He did not give into man's pride of life, but instead trusted in the One who gives life and provides abundantly.

STRIKE THREE, SATAN'S OUT!

When the devil had finished tempting Jesus, he left him until the next opportunity came (Luke 4:13).

Satan will try any and all things to tempt us, so do not fall into the deception that you are immune to something you don't currently struggle with. As soon as pride sets in, the door is open for the enemy. Here, Satan realized he lost this battle, but he wouldn't give up. He would wait for another "favorable time", just like he will with us. We must remain on guard and be strong in the Word, especially about who and Whose we are!

Lessons Learned:
Our enemy prowls around waiting for a weak moment to attack.
We thwart His advances by boldly speaking God's Word.

And the Authority goes to...

And said to him, "To you I will give all this authority and their glory, for it
has been delivered to me, and I give it to whom I will (Luke 4:6).

In this scripture, Satan claims he has authority. In fact, he says it was "handed" over to him. Authority is defined as jurisdiction or the right to rule and enforce power. Is this true? Has Satan been given authority?

According to Genesis 1:26, God gave man authority over the world and all that was in it. This was God's intention. However, in the garden, man fell to the serpent's schemes and willingly handed his God-given authority to Satan. That is what Satan is referring to in Luke 4:6. Satan had authority, but only because of man's choice and God's allowance for a period of time.

God's plan from the beginning was to reconcile and restore man to Himself through Jesus Christ. This restoration included authority over the creep's schemes. Through His crucifixion, Jesus defeated the power of sin. Through His resurrection, Jesus defeated death. Through His ascension, Jesus reclaimed our authority while all along revealing Himself as the ultimate Authority.

Now he (Christ) is far above any ruler or authority or power or leader or
anything else—not only in this world but also in the world to come
(Ephesians 1:21, NIRV).

Because Jesus lives *in* us and we are included *in* Him, we have been given *His* power and authority. This gift Adam handed over in the garden has been returned and magnified. It is now available to us, *if* we will reclaim it.

Reclaim your God-given authority

So you also are complete through your union with Christ, who is the head over every ruler and authority (Colossians 2:10).

Reclaim means to retrieve or recover something that was once yours. Will we take God at His Word and ask for an increase of faith in our authority through Christ? This authority was meant to be and is already ours. However, if you don't believe it, you will live like you don't have it.

CHANGE YOUR PERSPECTIVE

We've talked a lot about perspective and how important having the right one is. A correct perspective of the battle is vital for victory. A worldly perspective looks through foggy lenses and sees mankind as helpless pawns being played out in a universal chess match between two parallel opponents. Some days (or moves), Satan gets the upper hand and appears to be winning, while other days (or moves) God appears to be on top.

We need to change our perspective of this "chess match" to a Kingdom one. God is ALWAYS on top, and, because of Jesus' checkmate, *it is finished*. We are no longer pawns. We are royalty, powerful vessels full of the Holy Spirit and equipped to overcome the dark horse. And let's talk about these two opponents. It's no contest. It's like the reigning world champion playing against the high school chess club. And through Jesus, we are no longer just a chess piece. We get to participate in this epic match!

Our strategy involves no longer thinking *horizontally*, as though good and evil are on the same level playing field and we don't know the ending. Instead, we need to think *vertically* and open our eyes to the Truth. Satan's power (the creation) cannot be compared to God's (the creator). In fact, Satan's power cannot be compared to our power when we are *in* Christ. This fallen angel's power is no match for those who are made in the likeness and image of God. He is no match for those who call upon the name of Jesus and exercise their God-given power and authority.

ACCEPT YOUR CALLING

"The coming of the Son of Man can be illustrated by the story of a man going on a long trip. When he left home, he gave each of his slaves instructions about the work they were to do, and he told the gatekeeper to watch for his return" (Mark 13:34, NLT).

We were chosen, not just to be God's children, but also His ambassadors reconciling the world back to Him. Generally speaking, we all have the same calling; to shine with Him brightly so others can see. Shining for Him is not speaking of good works we should try to accomplish, but instead, remaining focused and full of Him so He gets all the glory for the extraordinary work He performs through those who are willing. When this happens, faith increases, because there is no doubt it's His great power at work.

Your eyes saw my unformed body; all the days ordained for me were written in your book before one of them came to be (Psalm 139:16, NIV).

We are all called to shine for Jesus. But we've also been personally chosen to fulfill a unique mission. God has numbered your days before you were even born. You will not leave this world any moment sooner than what God has planned. While God can do all things without us, He is generously giving us amazing opportunities to participate in His work!

Daniel, of the Old Testament, had a calling to share the visions God gave him. This calling, just like ours, comes with a responsibility; clinging to God, trusting only Him and giving Him all the glory. This call also comes with a resistance, a spiritual one. In chapter 10, Daniel fasted and mourned about a specific vision for three weeks with no response from God. Finally, an angel appeared with news.

> *Then he said to me, "Fear not, Daniel, for from the first day that you set your heart to understand and humbled yourself before your God, your words have been heard, and I have come because of your words. The prince of the kingdom of Persia withstood me twenty-one days, but Michael, one of the chief princes, came to help me, for I was left there with the kings of Persia,* (Daniel 10:12-13, emphasis mine).

God heard Daniel's persistent and humble prayer. Why did it take three weeks for Daniel to receive an answer? This scripture reveals a spiritual fight in the heavenly realms was blocking the message. A battle so strong the archangel Michael was called in to intervene. Regardless of the events occurring in another realm, Daniel remained steadfast doing His part; prayer.

The Bible gives us no reason to believe that this same partnership between the physical and spiritual no longer happens. Makes me wonder what is going on in the spiritual realm right now as you walk through this book. What could we be capable of if only we were aware?

God has created each of us uniquely and wonderfully, and He has placed you exactly where you are, at this time for a purpose. His purpose. This calling is specific to you. You are in partnership with Him. Your calling cannot be compared to anyone else's, because there is no one else like you. Ask for wisdom and discernment of your role in this battle.

Lesson Learned:
Since you're still breathing, there is something God wants to do through you.

And they have conquered him (Satan) by the blood of the Lamb and by the word of their testimony, for they loved not their lives even unto death (Revelation 12:11).

God uses all things for His good purposes. Your calling usually will come from an area you are passionate about, and most likely it's birthed from an area of struggle you have already or are currently walking through. Often times, it's your testimony God is calling you to share to one or many who are in similar situations. Our stories play a significant role in battle!

Ever since that day in Togo, West Africa, God has awakened me to my calling. He has placed a passion in me to first, encourage others who struggle with defeated thinking, and second, share the Truth. Our Lord Jesus and His Word can overcome anything we face.

Accept Your Responsibility

When I was in the thick of battle (deep in depression and unable to see a way out) and even sometimes today, I find myself crying out for God to take my struggles away and make life easier. What I've realized is, not only has He equipped me to walk through my struggles, He also wants to see me exercise my faith to overcome them.

He lifted me out of the slimy pit, out of the mud and mire; he set my feet on a rock and gave me a firm place to stand (Psalm 40:2, NIV).

I would remain in my "pit", not because Jesus didn't care, or His Word wasn't true; but because I had a responsibility and the ability to accomplish it by partnering with His Spirit. That is why He gave me the Holy Spirit and His authority, so I would exercise His great power. It makes so much more sense to me now.

Jesus is my Rock and firm footing I have been given.
In Him, I am free; not will be free, but already am free.

I must stand firm in this Truth and use my God-given authority to fight for that freedom that is already mine. That is the responsibility of my calling! And yours too. Not to shy away from battle and ask God to do it for us when our identity is questioned or when we feel weak and powerless.

But instead, follow Jesus' example in Luke 4:

- Boldly oppose the enemy's accusations out loud and command him to leave.
- Cast out the enemy's lies by speaking what is written.
- Demolish lies by proclaiming God's Word with our God-given authority.

As an extended branch of God's Army, we have been given a responsibility to reign in this life. Jesus has returned our right to reign and then some. Through the Holy Spirit, we have all the power we need to overcome the enemy's advances. Does a soldier just sit back and ask his commander to do all the work for him? No, that's why the soldier trains and learns offense and defense strategies; so he can put them into action.

Believers, we are called to put on our armor, go out into the trenches and use our weapon, the Word. Victory comes through faith. Remind the enemy who you are, and because of Christ, he has no power or authority over God's children.

EXERCISE YOUR SPIRITUAL AUTHORITY

Spiritual conflict is real and present. Unseen powers of this dark world are clashing with God's angels in the battle between good and evil. While we cannot physically see what's going on, we can definitely feel the repercussions of spiritual oppression and resistance. However, we don't have to live in fear or defeat.

218 | THE BELIEVER'S BATTLE STRATEGY

- Just like Elisha in 2 Kings 6, we must boldly pray with authority for eyes to see and divine intervention when faced with the impossible.
- Just like Daniel, we must remain steadfast in prayer when we're not hearing from God.
- Just as Jesus, throughout the gospels, continuously spoke against spiritual resistance present around Him, so must we.
- Just like when Jesus was tempted in the Wilderness, we must boldly speak God's Word against the enemy and command him to leave by the authority given.
- Just like Jesus' disciples in Luke 9 were called to cast out demons and heal, so must we step out in faith and fulfill our missions.

We are all called to this same bold authority when faced with spiritual "push back". I've seen firsthand the power of doing so.

I am not from a charismatic background, nor have I witnessed the casting out of demons. Even though it is spoken of often in the Bible, it had always seemed surreal to me. However, on mission trips while in other countries, my eyes have been opened to spiritual oppression. I used to rationalize *this is only in other parts of the world, not America*. The Truth is, that same resistance is in America. It just looks different, which makes it harder to identify.

When I stepped out to begin my writing for *The Believer's Battle Strategy*, I went through a season of severe oppression. I can't really explain it other than I was discontent, spiritually disconnected and tremendously discouraged. I couldn't physically write a single word. It was obvious to me a spiritual component was at play. I decided enough was enough and called in reinforcements.

A battle buddy listened and came right over. When she arrived, she could feel the oppressive heaviness present and began praying for the blood of Jesus to cover my home and my family. I began to feel lighter as she spoke Truth into me.

That afternoon I felt the oppressiveness return and I reached out to another spiritual warrior who in the past had joined me in battle for my family and home. She came over, prayed with bold confidence and spoke some of the very same things my battle buddy had. That was no coincidence, because it's the same Spirit living inside both of them. It's also the same Spirit that lives inside of me.

He wanted me to know He was right there, and it was time for me to use that same power and authority to keep this oppression away for good. That afternoon I began writing and a raging river of words flowed out. I haven't stopped since.

I've had other spiritually eye-opening experiences, and I'm sure many of you have as well. Each time the supernatural occurs, I find myself amazed saying, "This stuff *is* real." Of course it's real. But as time passes I find myself, just like the Old Testament Israelites, asking for further proof as a reminder.

The enemy is always up to something. To stay on guard, I don't place my focus on him, but I remain aware. I try and not let much time pass without praying over my family. I also keep Christian music (full of God's Word) playing throughout my home. This is my responsibility and as I step out in faith, God gives me His power and authority.

> While power means the *ability* to rule,
> authority means the *right* to rule.

As children of God, made complete in Christ, we have been given all the ability and right to reign in this life. We have been given the means to overcome and have victory over the enemy. But just like our other gifts, we have to choose it by believing, reclaiming and exercising our gift!

Conclusion

Jesus' wilderness experience is His example for us to follow when tempted or under attack. Jesus didn't have to speak the Word aloud, because He is God. I believe He did this to model how we must battle because we are not. We need to boldly speak God's Word against the lies we hear and in His name command the enemy to leave when we feel his presence.

Christ's victory will come regardless, but God is giving us the opportunity to participate in it. He also wants us to experience victory in this life by joining Him in:

- Planting spiritual seeds in the lost and hurting
- Interceding in prayer for others
- Living on purpose and out loud

While your eternal victory is secure, daily victory in your life will not come unless you first believe in your power and authority and second, exercise it. Daily remind yourself WHO He is and WHO you are because of it. Your power and authority is only as strong as your belief in it.

The enemy is banking on you not believing in or exercising your God-given power and authority. Will you use it?

BATTLE ORDERS
Ch 14 - Reclaim Authority

TAKE AWAYS

1.

2.

3.

REFLECTION:

1. What keeps you from following Jesus' example when you hear lies running through your mind, when you feel yourself losing your Spiritual Fruit, or you feel an unexplainable heaviness and oppression?
2. What keeps you from speaking God's Word aloud to counter an assault?
3. What keeps you from believing you have Christ's same authority?
4. What authority have you given over to the enemy?

Record Truths that challenge your findings
in your Truth Binder and speak them aloud.

BATTLE TOOL: Pray (Exercise your God-given Authority

1. Proclaim your God-given authority and come against the enemy's plans for your life.
2. Speak God's Word out loud in prayer!

Example:

Father, I believe I am a beloved child of God. I have been crucified with Christ, therefore it is no longer I living, but Christ in me. I now speak against Satan and all of his work coming against me, my family, my calling and the church. Satan, there is no place for you here and you must leave in the mighty name of Jesus. (You can specify the ways and attacks here) I now come against <u>fill in the blank</u> (fear, anxiety, oppression, anger, discontentment, discouragement, etc.). *Greater is He who is in me than he who is in the world. Christ has given me all the power I need to defeat, banish, and reject you and all your efforts. I am covered by the blood of Jesus and you must leave. Jesus, thank you for your power, authority and victory. I give you full reign in my life. Amen.*

1. Form a habit of using your authority and watch what happens. (i.e. reclaim authority over your home.)
2. Be sure to journal your experience. Our flesh needs constant reminding!

*Go deeper verses from this chapter: John 2:16, 3:30, 16:33, 19:30; Matthew 4:1-11; Luke 4:1-13, Mark 1:12-13; Galatians 2:20; Ephesians 1:13; Romans 5:17.

15

BATTLE LIKE YOU BELIEVE

Submit yourselves therefore to God. Resist the devil, and he will flee from you

.

— JAMES 4:7

WHEN FACED WITH A DILEMMA OR DECISION

What are you going to do? How are you going to fix this?

Often, amidst circumstance, thoughts like these hit me like a drippy faucet. And when others find out about my situation, "What are you going to do?" is either asked or implied. Now, imagined or not, I have an audience waiting to see what I will do.

My pulse will begin to race as my mind anxiously searches for a solution. I have this need to please others. It physically hurts me to let someone down. This pressure often causes me to shift into overdrive, jump into the "driver's seat" and head on a solo mission to figure out how to physically fix my situation because *that is what I'm supposed to do.*

Life is not as it seems. Most often, what the world tells us is the opposite of God's intent and plan. Satan has twisted so many concepts that we've seen in past chapters such as love, abundance and strongholds. In this chapter, we will add a few more beginning with how to fight.

- Our *battle* is <u>not</u> in the physical realm.
- Our *enemy* is <u>not</u> who is standing in front of us or looking back at us in the mirror.
- Our *fight* is <u>not</u> with people or our circumstances.
- Our *fighting* is <u>not</u> to be done impulsively or in the flesh.

Yes, we are to fight proactively, but what are we to do *first*? Matthew 6:33 says, *But seek first the kingdom of God and his righteousness, and all these things will be added to you.*

First, we are to trust that God is in control and seek Him for the answers. Seeking God and His perspective *first* is action that must be done intentionally. If we don't, our focus will be on the world, its perspective and the temporary and counterfeit solutions.

Fear Like Jehoshaphat

In this chapter, we will learn the Matthew 6:33 principle from an Old Testament king of Judah, King Jehoshaphat. It wasn't originally his nature to seek God first. Let's face it, our flesh wants no part of that.

Jehoshaphat had previously struggled with the approval of man over God. He was a good man taught well by his father King Asa; however, he had a habit of compromising because of his need to please others. He permitted idols to remain in the land, and allowed man to determine his plans instead of listening to God.

Can I be honest? I also struggle with this. No, I don't allow these same kinds of "idols" to remain in my home, but there are things and people I put before God. Sometimes I also hold back from being, saying and doing all God created for me out of fear of what others might think. Impatience and doubt will often cause me to jump in head first or ask others how to fix a problem without first consulting God or waiting for His answer.

For am I now seeking the approval of man, or of God? Or am I trying to please man? If I were still trying to please man, I would not be a servant of Christ (Galatians 1:10).

Ouch! This makes my sin no different than King Jehoshaphat's. The root of my sin is misplaced fear; something I've struggled with for a long time. While it's gotten better as I've matured, if I look close enough, it's still present.

Several times the Bible tells us *not* to place our fear in man, the world or circumstances. Rather, we are to have a fear of the Lord. It's important to note we are not to fear in the way the world perceives fear, but instead, with a reverence, awe and trust in God and His plans. King David, a man after God's own heart, and King Solomon, the wisest of men, both claimed fearing the Lord is the beginning, or foundation of wisdom.

What we fear is an indicator of where our worship, respect and trust lie. We are to only act in fear of God, not man. King Jehoshaphat learned this valuable lesson. In fact, he recognized the severity of it and appointed judges to help bring this message to all of Judah.

And he charged them: "Thus you shall do in the fear of the Lord, *in faithfulness, and with your whole heart* (2 Chronicles 19:9).

Lesson Learned:
We can't have it both ways. We either fear God or man.

Fight Like Jehoshaphat

2 Chronicles 20 presents us with a great example on how to fight in the midst of battle. While King Jehoshaphat's specific circumstance was an actual impending war, we can all apply his same strategy to life's circumstances, both big and small. We pick up this story with King Jehoshaphat realizing a vast army was rapidly approaching to fight.

Could God have been testing the king on what he had just learned? Possibly. This is no easy test, for it would instill fear into anyone receiving this kind of news. Would Jehoshaphat place his fear in the incoming attack (man) or His sovereign Creator (God)? Would he immediately get to work listening to the strategies and plans of his military leaders (man), or would he first stop, seek and listen to His Commanding Officer (God)?

> Then Jehoshaphat was afraid and set his face to seek the Lord, and proclaimed a fast throughout all Judah (2 Chronicles 20:3).

King Jehoshaphat passed the test. In the midst of fear and chaos, he made the difficult and right choice. In fact, it was so against his nature, he had to *resolve himself* and *set his mind* to seek the Lord alone. He went through the same inner struggles we do today when faced with difficult circumstances and decisions. In fact, he had a whole nation looking and asking, *What are you going to do?* Now that's a lot of pressure!

King Jehoshaphat had his flaws just like we all do, but here he made the right choice. Instead of reacting in fear of his circumstances, he responded with reverence and trust in God who is over the circumstance. And he stepped out boldly and declared for all of Judah to do the same. He was no longer worried about what others would think. I'm sure there were many critics among the crowd, but Jehoshaphat either couldn't see them or chose to ignore them because his focus was on God instead of man.

The story continues with Jehoshaphat remaining in a posture of prayer for help and guidance. He learned this had to be his first line of defense. Have you ever said the words, *I don't know what else to do; I guess I'll just pray?* I've been guilty of it. I now see the father of lies all over that one. We have been de-sensitized to the true power and purpose of prayer. What we're actually saying is, "God, I can't trust you with this. I have to do something."

Lesson Learned:
Prayer is our first defense, especially when afraid or in battle.

Pray like Jehoshaphat

When Jehoshaphat began to pray, he didn't go straight to the point of asking for help. Instead, he sought hard after God and spent several verses praising and worshipping the Lord; reminding the Almighty of His power, His goodness and all the great things He had already done.

Now, did God need this reminding? Of course not. But King Jehoshaphat did. Meditating on and speaking of how great God is built up Jehoshaphat's faith. It filled him with the courage and peace of God's sovereignty. Only then did Jehoshaphat present his requests to the only One who could save.

How long did he stay in this posture of prayer? As long as it took.

> Then the Spirit of the LORD came on Jahaziel son of Zechariah ...as he stood in the assembly. He said: "Listen, King Jehoshaphat and all who live in Judah and Jerusalem! This is what the LORD says to you: 'Do not be afraid or discouraged because of this vast army. For the battle is not yours, but God's (2 Chronicles 20:14-15, NIV, emphasis mine).

The Lord speaks in many ways; through a knowing in your heart, the Word or even other people. Truth tellers. In this story, the prophet Jahaziel had great news of reassurance and the Lord's strategy. This battle was not their battle to fight. It was God's.

> *You will not have to fight this battle. Take up your positions; stand firm and see the deliverance the* LORD *will give you, Judah and Jerusalem. Do not be afraid; do not be discouraged. Go out to face them tomorrow, and the* LORD *will be with you'"* (2 Chronicles 20:17, NIV).

After receiving this promise from God, Jehoshaphat didn't delay his worship for what was to come. Instead, he remained in a posture of prayer, praise and expectancy *before* he saw any physical sign of victory. Yes, this is an unconventional way to fight in the world's eyes, but Jehoshaphat believed His God would come through!

Lesson Learned:
Defense is praising God even in the uncertainty or worst of situations.

God's Soldiers

We are to fight opposite from the world. If we're looking at our circumstance with worldly lenses, our strategy appears foolish and complacent. However, Kingdom lenses will reveal something much different; victory.

Before battle, a soldier receives his training, uniform and weapons. He is then sent out on mission. He does not act without specific orders, and he definitely doesn't come up with his own. His job is to stand firm and defend until he receives further orders. This is exactly what Jehoshaphat did and what we are called to do.

As Jehoshaphat placed his trust in his Creator, all of Judah and Jerusalem bowed down in worship. They continued in their orders to pray without ceasing and give thanks in all things. Jehoshaphat even appointed the infantry, his front lines, to remain in this posture during battle. That is courageous faith!

Watch what happens next.

> *As they began to sing and praise, the* LORD *set ambushes against the men of Ammon and Moab and Mount Seir who were invading Judah, and they were defeated* (2 Chronicles 20:22, NIV).

God's plans never fail,
no matter how outrageous they seem!

Not only were Judah's enemies defeated, they destroyed one another while Jehoshaphat's army remained in a posture of praise and worship. God told them they were not to fight but to stand firm and take their position of prayer. No further orders were needed in this particular battle. They didn't allow the world to distract, instead they chose to obey even when they couldn't see the outcome or make sense of it.

Lesson Learned:
Approach God during battle with a Jehoshaphat faith, trust and expectancy!

There are many soldiers from the Bible that displayed the same faith as Jehoshaphat.

MOSES. In Exodus, he led the Israelites out of Egypt as Pharaoh's army aggressively pursued. The Israelites complained in fear, but Moses by faith encouraged them with the same prophesied words in Exodus

14:13, *Don't be afraid, stand still and watch the Lord rescue you*. This time, however, God gave the Israelites further orders to act on; keep stepping forward in faith. As they obeyed, God parted the Red Sea.

JOSHUA. In Joshua 6, Moses' predecessor was given offensive orders to take over the City of Jericho. Joshua and his army were to march around Jericho for seven days with the Ark of the Covenant, while rams' horns and trumpets were to be blown on the final lap. These were their orders, once again outrageous in the world's eyes; but miraculously, it brought down the city's walls.

ELISHA. In 2 Kings, as previously mentioned, the prophet was being surrounded by a vast army. He knew his battle orders were to stand firm in a posture of prayer as the Lord's army delivered them from harm. Elisha's prayer, as well as ours, is an essential part of battle.

Why are these stories so important? Because God was the *only* explanation for these incredible victories.

- Each was faced with a unique battle that brought on fear.
- Each chose to fear God instead of man.
- Each looked spiritually, listened for God's orders and proceeded obediently.
- Each fully yielded and sought after the Lord. Then, and only then, were they equipped to follow through with the orders given in their specific circumstances which led to victory.

There was no question *Who* fought and *Who* won the battles. Man could not take credit, for the glory of the Lord was on full display.

Lesson Learned:
God will fight my battles if I let Him. God, give me a willing,
surrendered, and obedient heart like Moses, Joshua, and Elisha.

You will not need to Fight in this Battle

I am tired of the pressure and exhausting task of figuring out how to keep everything together. This statement that *we will not need to fight* is a breath of fresh air, because it reminds me none of this is my job. I am God's ambassador sent out to simply represent. I was never meant to come up with the plan or be self-sufficient in it. We have to be so careful of this deception.

We are to reflect God's glory, not take it. We need to get out of His way and humbly admit our need for Him to fight for us. God wants to fight our battles, but He needs us to stop taking the lead and hand Him the reins. Please note, this is not a free pass for complacency. We are to seek Him and await further orders.

Be still, and know that I am God; I will be exalted among the nations, I will be exalted in the earth! (Psalm 46:10).

Why is God telling us to stop fighting? Why are we to *be still*? An obvious answer would be because God knows what's best and wants us to hear Him. But I believe the answer is much bigger. The very next verse says the Lord of Heaven's Armies are with us and God is our fortress. God wants to prove His faithfulness. He wants to remind us of His power and strength. And lastly, He wants His glory revealed to the world.

Lesson Learned:
Christ cannot be seen in self-sufficiency.

Our Winning Strategy

Both Old and New Testament believers have gone before us implementing God's foolproof strategy. Each story resulted in miraculous testimony and faith being increased because of it.

The Apostle Paul, who endured years of suffering for Christ time and time again, remained content in all things. John, Jesus' disciple, saw God's power on full display as his life was miraculously spared in the midst of boiling tar. And who can forget Jesus' testimony to us while in the Wilderness? Each story revealed God's goodness and glory.

Each story is unique; however, each victory
came from the same consistent strategy.

STEP 1: SURRENDER

Take up your position...(2 Chronicles 20:17, NIV).

Submit yourselves, then to God... (James 4:7, NIV).

We fight and overcome in the battle by taking a position of surrender. I know it sounds like an oxymoron, but remember God thinks differently than the world. Who are we actually surrendering to anyway? God; not the enemy. We are surrendering so we can decrease and His work and power in us may increase. We are merely jumping into the passenger seat and allowing our Commander to take over His vessel.

Submitting to God means coming before Him in humility and trust, recognizing His way is best. In its context, James' letter was written to Christians caught up in the world's ways and wisdom. Falling prey to this deception results in pride. In the same sense, when we seek to figure out and fix things on our own, we are succumbing to pride.

God opposes the proud but gives grace to the humble (James 4:6, NIV).

Putting on humility is no simple task, but when we do, grace abounds. He promises perfect and constant peace regardless of the battle we're facing.

Remaining in a position of prayer and praise while following our standing orders found in God's Word is key to winning the battle. To receive further orders of direct instruction, I must remain in constant communication with my Commander. Positioning myself to seek God requires reading the Word, prayer and "armoring up" daily.

Seeking God is rejecting your thoughts despite your feelings, including fear, and the world's solutions. Instead, it's putting on the mind of Christ and focusing on His promises and perspective. It's a moment-by-moment surrender to your plans, expectations and agenda in exchange for His.

STEP 2: WAIT AND DEFEND

...stand firm (2 Chronicles 20:17, NIV).

...resist the devil (James 4:7, NIV).

It's only with a renewed mind that we are able to wait defensively. Keeping our minds set on God and standing firm on our Rock is taking the defensive approach of a soldier while God works the offense. Defense is the act of resisting attack. Our orders are to defend and resist while we wait expectantly for either further instruction or victory. Again, this is not complacency; it's eagerly waiting for what's to come while remaining in proactive defense mode.

Our standing defense orders are to remain in the Bible (our Word Weapon) and focus on God (our Victor). The Word is your life blood for every situation especially in the waiting. And your Savior is your blood covering from the enemy especially in discouraging and painful seasons.

While we will spend much of our life waiting, it is possible to walk through trials and hard seasons with peace and joy. In fact, this is one of the reasons Jesus came; so we may experience the fullness of Him especially in the waiting and suffering. Even Isaiah of the Old Testament prophesied of this Truth.

> *But they who wait for the* LORD *shall renew their strength; they shall mount up with wings like eagles, they shall run and not be weary; they shall walk and not faint* (Isaiah 40:31).

Waiting is not a bad thing, especially when we know how to resist the enemy. God has fully equipped us with *weapons* to wait.

Lesson Learned:
God uses our waiting to refine, stretch and build up our spiritual muscles.

Waiting Weapons

Do you ever wonder how some people are able to keep their peace even in the toughest of times? They have learned how to battle God's way. These waiting weapons give us our practical "how to" on fighting back in the waiting. When faced with temptation, discouragement, impatience or oppression; put your spiritual artillery into action.

PRAYER. This fierce weapon should always be our first line of defense no matter what. Prayer has many more facets to it than just pleading our wants. It is communicating with the only One who is always there and will never let you down. It is direct contact with the One who knows best. The more time you spend with Him, the more your wants and desires will miraculously become His.

We need to pray His Word and promises not as empty words or repetition, but to remind and build up our faith. We need to pray first and continually, not just when nothing else is working, but at all times so we can unleash our God-given power and authority over the enemy's plans.

SPEAKING THE WORD. When wrong thoughts and fears invade, God's Word offers our counterattack. Speaking the Word is a force multiplier serving two purposes. First, speaking Truth brings life, healing and freedom to those who hear and place their trust in it. Second, speaking Truth is lifting our Faith Shield and deflecting the enemy's advances to steal, kill and destroy. The enemy has to obey God's Word.

THANKSGIVING. In the midst of sorrow, indifference or self-pity; thanksgiving is revolutionary. It pulls us out of the "all about me" perspective and redirects our focus onto God's goodness. Being thankful is not a feeling, it's Truth. We have so much to be thankful for, even in the very trials we are walking through. The enemy likes to fog up our lenses so we forget and live only by what we can see. Thankfulness reminds us of the unseen. There is so much more to this life and the one to come.

WORSHIP. It's showing reverence and adoration for something. We were created for worship, which explains why we are always worshiping something. Think about it: if we are not focusing our worship on God regardless of the activity, then we have directed it towards something or someone else (i.e. ourself). Imagine the spiritual repercussions if we'd keep God as our focus of worship in spite of what's going on.

OBEDIENCE. It's an act of worship. The enemy likes to deceive our hearts so our motives to obey are out of fear or to get what we want. When these are our motives, obedience is short-lived and not pleasing to the Lord. True obedience can only come out of love and is only possible when God's power is involved. Also, unconfessed sin or disobedience can become what keeps us in a holding pattern. Check your heart and motives. Often God is the one waiting. He's waiting for us to surrender something.

Lesson Learned:
Exercising my waiting weapons especially when
my flesh does not want to builds tremendous faith.

STEP 3 - BREAKTHROUGH

...and see the deliverance the Lord will give you (2 Chronicles 20:17, NIV).

...and he (devil) will flee from you (James 4:7, NIV).

The final step is the finish line, where we see God at work. Our Jericho walls will crumble. The troubling waters will part. The enemy will turn on itself or flee. Here is where physical or spiritual healing occurs, and God reveals His sovereignty. When believers battle God's way – through worship, thankfulness, surrender and obedience – the Almighty's splendor is on full display.

Lesson Learned:
When I battle God's way the devil has no other choice but to flee.

Conclusion

Let us not become weary in doing good, for at the proper time we will reap a harvest if we do not give up (Galatians 6:9).

God is always working, especially in the waiting. Most likely, you are currently waiting for something. If you are not experiencing joy in the wait:

- Check your thinking
- Shift your perspective.
- Fight with your waiting weapons.
- Seek God for further orders
- Expect victory.

Your Heavenly Father desires to pour out His blessings on you and give you the desires of your heart. He wants you to be more than an overcomer, but what He desires most is for you to continue *being transformed into his image with ever-increasing glory, which comes from the Lord, who is the Spirit* (2 Corinthians 3:18).

Trust and worship while you wait for breakthrough.

BATTLE ORDERS
Ch 15- Battle Like You Believe

TAKE AWAYS

1.

2.

3.

REFLECTION:

1. What is your default response when faced with difficult circumstance (i.e. go into fix-it mode, seek out others, etc.)? Give a current or recent example.
2. What is your tendency in the midst of difficult decision-making (i.e. people pleasing, control, self-sufficiency, etc.)? Give a current or recent example.
3. What specific thing(s) are you waiting on or for right now?
4. How might you be getting in the way and preventing God from fighting your battles?
5. What steps can you take today to respond like King Jehoshaphat?

*Go deeper verses in this chapter: Acts 13:22; 1 Kings 4:30; Psalm 11:10; Proverbs 9:10; Romans 8:37; Isaiah 26:3, James 1:2-4.

BATTLE TOOL: Worship (Waiting Weapons)

Rejoice always, pray without ceasing, give thanks in all circumstances; for this is the will of God in Christ Jesus for you (1 Thessalonians 5:16-18).

1. REJOICE ALWAYS: Rejoicing in all things comes out of a heart of joyful praise and adoration through worship. Romans 12:1 (NIV) says because of His great mercy, *offer your bodies as a living sacrifice, holy and pleasing to God – this is your true and proper worship.* Worship is not just church attendance, reading the Bible, or even prayer. It's moment-by-moment sacrificial living. Practically speaking, worship is inviting our Victor into each day; and seeking to honor Him in all we think, do or say.

Battle Action:

1. Think on God's goodness by meditating on His Word daily.
2. Proclaim God's goodness by speaking the Word out loud in faith daily.
3. Praise Him by listening to hymns and singing His promises.
4. Plead for a heart of obedience as you seek out to follow his precepts and promptings.

2. PRAY CONTINUALLY: Prayer should always be our first line of defense, but unfortunately is often used as a last resort. Do you have a tendency towards self-sufficiency? Stop and repent. Then choose to trust and seek His instruction.

Battle Action:

1. The next time you are faced with a situation, decision or dilemma; stop immediately and pray. (Pray before the thought *I don't know what to do* even has time to come into your mind).
2. Listen to your prayers (write them down if it helps.) Which

perspective are you choosing as you pour your heart out to the Father?

3. Change your prayers from a worldly (all about me) perspective to a Kingdom (loving God and others) one by speaking God's Word (about His sovereignty, love and promises) as you pray. Watch your faith grow and heart's desire follow.

3. GIVE THANKS IN ALL CIRCUMSTANCES: There is so much to be thankful for. Even if you're in the "pit" and nothing comes to mind, *consider it pure joy, whenever you face trials of many kinds, because you know that the testing of your faith produces perseverance* (James 1:2-3). If you can force your flesh to choose right perspective in the moment, you are calling out the enemy's bluff and he will not know what to do. With thanksgiving, believe in God's promises instead of Satan's forebodings. With thanksgiving, focus on God instead of the circumstance, on Truth instead of wrong thinking.

Battle Action:

1. Create a personal thankfulness list. God has given you a plethora of blessings (tangible and intangible) we often take for granted. Whether it's the feel of sunshine, the ability to breathe, the new job, the new friend, the great tasting lunch, the smile from the coffee barista, etc.; challenge yourself to come up with at least ten a day for one week.
2. When you can't see anything to be thankful for, choose a posture of thankfulness by reciting James 1:2-3 from above. Thankfulness in the midst of your "junk" opens your eyes to a Kingdom perspective, but also how He loves and cares for you individually.
3. Share your list with a battle buddy to help boost more blessing ideas.
4. Continually add to your list and read aloud when self-pity, doubt or impatience try to take over.

16

BATTLE LIKE JESUS

Jesus said to them, "My food is to do the will of him who sent me and to accomplish his work."

— JOHN 4:34

THE BOOT CAMP JOURNEY

I have learned much from Bible greats like King Jehoshaphat. I now see my role in battle is to pursue my Commander and the specific orders He's given me. I now see that fighting victoriously is choosing a hopeful and expectant position in prayer while waiting for God's perfectly-timed victory. But what about those times when I can't see as clearly or when the battle isn't as obvious? This is where my perfectionist tendencies can be a good thing. While I know I can't be perfect, I still want to learn as much as I can from the Perfect One.

Through the gospel letters (Matthew, Mark, Luke and John), Jesus modeled the life of an expert soldier. Before He even came to earth,

Jesus knew His mission; and in order to fulfill it He knew His flesh had to seek hard after His Father for strength. His specific orders were humanly impossible, but of the upmost importance. In fact, they were a matter of life and death for all. Jesus could've chosen to change the plan because He is in fact God. But, He did not waver in His necessary mission to save mankind.

Pray Like Jesus

But Jesus often withdrew to lonely places and prayed (Luke 5:16, NIV).

Intimacy with His Father was priority. Jesus was fully God, but He was also fully man. To rid Himself of the world's constant pull, He withdrew to renew *often*. If Jesus needed to renew in prayer, how much more should we yearn for this empowering manna daily?

In Matthew 6:6 (NIV), Jesus said, *But when you pray, go into your room, close the door and pray to your Father, who is unseen.* In other words, seek solitary time with your Father. He often modeled this instruction through scripture.

Jesus would sacrifice sleep for strength. Mark 1:35 shows how Jesus would wake early while it was still dark to seek solitude. This particular instance was following a busy day of both the physical and spiritual healing of many. Jesus had to have been exhausted from the day's activity, yet He recognized where true rest and renewal was found.

Jesus would seek complete comfort from His Father. Luke 6:12 tells of Jesus going to the mountainside and praying all night. In this particular instance, Jesus was facing the task of choosing His disciples (including Judas whom He knew would betray Him). Also, before His arrest, in Matthew 26, Jesus was found in the Garden of Gethsemane on His knees in earnest prayer while His disciples slept. In both instances, Jesus' heart was troubled, and the time was coming for courageous action. He knew prayer was the only answer.

I've learned there is no magic prayer formula to time with the Father. God just wants you. *All* of you. I want to be like Paul and seek a posture of prayer at all times. I want to be like Jesus and fully partake in this intimate, sacred union. To pray like Jesus, we have to create space and withdraw to solitary places.

Lesson Learned:
Solitude is not isolation, it's intimate time with the Heavenly Father.

Let Us Pray

God already knows what we need even before we ask. Yet, He wants us to come to Him each day and share our joys and deepest longings. Amazingly, God Almighty is also *Abba Father.* He wants to laugh and cry with us, and He also wants to gently lead and pour out His love. We allow Him to do this when we shift our focus away from the world and onto His Kingdom.

There are times, more than I'd like to admit, when I pray without my spiritual lenses. My prayer focus is for my problems to go away. I need a perspective shift, and this is a battle of its own. In Matthew 6:9-13, Jesus provides us with our *battle cry.*

"Our Father in heaven, hallowed be your name. Your kingdom come, your will be done, on earth as it is in heaven. Give us this day our daily bread, and forgive us our debts, as we also have forgiven our debtors. And lead us not into temptation, but deliver us from evil. For yours is the kingdom and the power and the glory, forever. Amen."

This is how we battle through prayer. Always begin with praise and worship of our Sovereign God. This softens our hearts to His will over our own. The Christian life is not about our problems going away, but how we can reflect Him in the midst of them. King Jehoshaphat did this with miraculous results and we can too.

As our faith builds and perspectives change, our requests will align to His. It is then that we *ask*, as well as *confess* and *repent* of our sins. Intimate prayer time ends just like it begins, with praise and worship. We need this constant reminding and assurance of Who's in charge and Who knows what's best. God wants to answer our requests, and always does with a "yes," when it's aligned with His will.

Time with the Father is not a list of rules, but instead rich intimacy. If we look at this time legalistically, we will fight inadequately. When Christianity becomes a "religion," our relationship diminishes and our battle efforts lose effectiveness.

Jesus' Battle Plan

Knowing our battle orders comes when we know God's Word. Hearing further orders comes with intimacy. These two components are crucial for victory as Jesus has perfectly demonstrated. In Luke 4, Jesus was led into the wilderness for solitude and preparation for His ministry. As previously mentioned, this was also where He defeated Satan's plan with strategy living.

QUOTE SCRIPTURE WHEN ATTACKED

Then Jesus said to him, "Be gone, Satan! For it is written, "'You shall worship the Lord your God and him only shall you serve'" (Matthew 4:10).

Just like the first Adam (and Eve), Satan came in for the kill by presenting Jesus (the last Adam) with questions to cause doubt of God's Word. Eve took the bait and began a whole inner dialogue with Satan resulting in doubt, confusion and pride. Adam and Eve both then committed acts of disobedience.

When faced with the same dilemma, Jesus, on the other hand, responded much differently. He recognized His need to not let His flesh entertain *any* ideas from the enemy. With each accusation, Jesus immediately combated the arrows by quoting scripture. The Bible states Jesus was weak, weary and incredibly hungry after fasting for forty days. In the battle, He set His focus on His Father, instead of His feelings, wants and desires. As the arrows continued, Jesus in His authority commanded Satan to leave.

Jesus modeled our James 4:7 winning strategy in the midst of physical weakness, temptation and direct attack. Fully surrendered to His Father, He resisted the devil and continued in defense mode using His Word Weapon until the enemy fled. We must follow suit. Don't just *say* the Word, but boldly proclaim it aloud with authority from Jesus.

Lesson Learned:
We have been given the same strategy as Christ.
It is imperative we use it!

SURRENDER TO THE HEAVENLY FATHER'S WILL

Do you not believe that I am in the Father and the Father is in me? The words that I say to you I do not speak on my own authority, but the Father who dwells in me does his works (John 14:10).

Jesus knew His specific calling was to save humanity, yet He still had the choice to follow through. For 33 years on earth, He remained patient, obedient and strictly about the Father's business. Jesus was fully God the Son, yet fully surrendered to God the Father. In fact, doing the Father's will was the nourishment that sustained Him.

While we cannot fully comprehend the Holy Trinity, we do know through scripture Christ is now living in all believers through the Holy Spirit. Stop for a moment and meditate on this Truth.

The Expert Soldier lives in you!

He will do the Father's good work through you *if* you allow. None of our stories will compare to Jesus's story, and yet we have been given His same power to persevere through the chapters of life.

Jesus knew what was to come (the waiting, hatred, rejection, betrayal, torture, anguish and brutal death); yet He still chose to fulfill His calling and bear the sins of the world. This was no easy task even for Him. In the garden, as He prayed in agony to prepare, His sweat became like drops of blood. Jesus then prayed using the same battle cry blueprint He handed down to us in Matthew 6.

"Father, if you are willing, take this cup from me; yet not my will, but yours be done" (Luke 22:42, NIV).

Jesus lifted His requests but surrendered them to His Father's will. Even to the point of death, He continued to pray for His Father's will over His fleshly comfort. He remained steadfast by keeping His focus on the bigger picture, God's Kingdom. With patience and humility, He continued living without sin waiting for His true mission to unfold. He knew the ending and the importance of His assignment.

Lesson Learned:
We know the ending; therefore, must remember
the importance of our assignment - the Great Commission.

JESUS WENT AROUND DOING GOOD

How God anointed Jesus of Nazareth with the Holy Spirit and with power. He went about doing good and healing all who were oppressed by the devil, for God was with him (Acts 10:38).

Jesus never took His eyes off His Father or what He was called to do. He was so full of His Father, who is Love, He couldn't be anything different. This *doing good* was a love for all and poured out in many ways.

How did Jesus love? Notice, He was first *anointed* with the Holy Spirit's power. He then remaining surrendered, obedient and aware of His Father's will. As a result, He was aware of and sensitive to the needs of others. He made Himself available for the divine appointments or love opportunities His Father placed in front of Him. At times, these appointments were inconvenient, but Jesus knew lives were at stake. So, He changed His plans often to tend to His people.

Did this take away from His mission? No, because ultimately, His mission was to redeem those whom His Father had given Him. From the children He blessed, the listeners who needed food, the sick and oppressed who needed healing, those who needed encouragement and those who needed correction (Yes, this is also love when done with the right motive); He was there and always offered His sacrificial love.

Jesus' spent His last days well-intentioned, preparing and modeling for us, His disciples, the way to glorify the Father:

He recognized and made time for divine appointments. The demon-possessed man, the restored girl and the bleeding woman were just a few recorded in Luke 8. No matter what His plans were for the day, He was always willing to change them for those who sought after Him in faith.

He made the most of every opportunity and put wisdom into action. He continually spoke Truth to His disciples, as well as the lost, about what was to come. In Colossians 4:5, Paul challenges us to do the same.

He poured out His love and humbly served. In a symbolic act of love and humility, He washed His disciples' feet. Our King took the job of the lowliest servant to spread God's Love which unconditionally shows no favorites.

He battled in prayer. At Gethsemane awaiting His arrest, He fervently pleaded for His Father's will over His own.

He urged His followers. Remain ready for the time is near. Also, *Watch and pray that you may not enter into temptation. The spirit indeed is willing, but the flesh is weak* (Matthew 26:41).

While we don't know when our last days will be, we do know where we are going. So, let's live our short lives on purpose. We are God's seed planters working the fields, and the harvest is ripe. If we are too busy and not sensitive to what God is doing around us, we will miss opportunities and the blessings they bring.

For we are God's handiwork, created in Christ Jesus to do good works, which God prepared in advance for us to do (Ephesians 2:10, NIV).

Have you noticed there is nobody out there quite like you? Each day we come across different personalities gifted in different ways to do different jobs. God's design was perfect and on purpose, so everything would be accomplished.

The church is the same. It is a body with many parts. God created man and woman with different temperaments and strengths to accomplish different missions all to help further His one purpose. He makes His vessels fit together perfectly as each does His special work. God has created each of us to do a special work. We were created for such a time as this.

Lesson Learned:
Jesus wants to continue His good work
through His willing and available vessels today.

Jesus lived a life of obedience

Jesus, fully man and fully God, went about doing good perfectly. In fact, John 21:25 says if every good thing He did was recorded, the whole world would not have room for the books that would be written. He never missed an opportunity to serve and He never veered off track into His own selfish desires. He never sinned or fell short.

No matter how hard we try, we cannot attain perfection. We can, however, live with a reverence and conviction to obey while we receive His love offering of grace and mercy when we fail. We are covered by the blood of Christ. His love covers a multitude of sins. In fact, it covers them all! It was for love that Christ came, and it was for life that He lived among us and gave Himself for us.

> *Jesus answered him, "If anyone loves me, he will keep my word, and my Father will love him, and we will come to him and make our home with him* (John 14:23).

In order to "do good", we must first love. Here, the ESV translation says to love is to *keep* (spiritually guard and properly maintain) God's Word. Remaining in the Word as it sets us free is the foundation of *The Believer's Battle Strategy.*

The NIV translation says to love is to *obey* the word or His commandments. In reading this, my works default makes me feel condemnation because in some way or another, I will daily fall short.

Does this mean I don't love God when I disobey? No, that is deception.

God's law began with Ten Commandments. Through Moses and the prophets, it evolved into over 600 rituals and rules to follow. The purpose of the law was not to condemn but to show us right from wrong, and that no one is capable of living up to it. Unfortunately, we often see the law as a measuring stick and are held captive to our performance.

Jesus, knowing He was the ultimate love offering, came to break this wall of deception. He lived love out loud and showed us the way. Through the Holy Spirit, He was coming to live in all believers and continue His ministry. Repeatedly, He has instructed us where to focus. When asked what the greatest commandment was, Jesus would answer with the 4-letter word – Love.

The Greatest Commandment

And he said to him, "You shall love the Lord your God with all your heart and with all your soul and with all your mind. This is the great and first commandment. And a second is like it: You shall love your neighbor as yourself. On these two commandments depend all the Law and the Prophets" (Matthew 22:37-40).

What is the greatest commandment? When asked, each time Jesus would answer to love God (Deuteronomy 6:5) and love your neighbor as yourself (Leviticus 19:18). In addition, He also addresses how obeying these two commands sum up all the commandments. I see now that if we are walking in love, then we are obeying. When Jesus speaks, we need to listen. When He repeats Himself, we need to take note. To love is to obey.

Love is a simple act which takes godly strength. In fact, it takes God. We are only capable of love when God, who is love, is allowed to come in and take over. It is God's love, not our counterfeit version mustered up in our own strength, that changes lives and radiates His glory. Let's cast out the imitation and replace it with the real thing that is completely counter cultural.

Our Greatest Weapon

Since Jesus says to love is the greatest commandment, it is safe to assume love is the greatest weapon we have at our disposal. If love is where God wants our focus to be, we can conclude that preventing or distracting us from loving is most likely an area of priority for the enemy. Conversely, when we put love into practice, especially when we don't feel like it, love becomes a weapon of mass destruction and a multiplier of faith!

Could this be why we go some days so consumed with our own stuff we cannot even see or muster up compassion for others hurting around us? Could this be why there is so much disunity, offense, bitterness, resentment and hurt in our relationships, especially among believers? This situation we all find ourselves in at some point has the enemy written all over it. What would happen if we all started battling with our greatest weapon?

If I have the gift of prophecy and can fathom all mysteries and all knowledge, and if I have a faith that can move mountains, but do not have love, I am nothing (1 Corinthians 13:2).

Here, Paul refers to just how important love is. Each of us has been given specific giftings as part of the body of Christ. However, all of us are given the ability and order to love. He cautions us about focusing on our gifts rather than love. He even goes to the extreme and says our gifts are worth nothing, no matter how great they are, if they are not done in love.

We can give everything we have to the poor, but it doesn't mean we love. This proves walking in love is a posture of the heart, not merely an outward action. It often includes outward actions; however, it must be accompanied with a pure motive.

The reality is our flesh doesn't feel like serving others especially when we have troubles of our own. Sometimes our motives are not what they need to be, but we can still choose to put love into action anyway. Remember, we are training our flesh to let our spirits lead and our goal is to form life habits. When we continue to take a posture of surrender and choose love in action, our hearts will follow.

Lesson Learned:
Increase your God power by serving others,
especially when you don't feel like it.

Conclusion

Battling like Jesus is our perfect strategy! When we find ourselves surrounded by struggle, it's hard to look outward and empathize with the rest of the world, or even just the people you live with. The enemy wants us to remain inner-focused so he can wreak havoc on us as well as those we love. Don't allow Satan to make your greatest weapon inoperative.

Some days, more than I would like to admit, I become a victim to this. However, I can testify to what happens when you add love to a situation. Love is choosing to look outward with a Kingdom perspective.

When we do this, we'll begin to see a world desperately in need of and searching for God. We will begin to see love opportunities God has placed all around. We will begin to have a heart to help others and it will become refreshing nourishment as it takes our focus away from our circumstances. Reap the blessings of blessing others.

Putting love into action especially when you first get this is like a gut punch to the enemy. It's a game changer. He wants you to stay focused on all the ways you're disobeying the law, so you continue to focus inwardly and on improving yourself. He wants you to stay focused on the ways you've been wronged and the people behind it.

The commandment to love completely shifts the focus outward and maximizes impact. In stepping out selflessly, especially when we don't feel like it, not only are we winning the battles, we're helping others towards victory.

In Jesus, we have been given abundantly more than we can even ask or imagine. Not only is He our Redeemer, He is also our Perfect Example to follow. He has given us everything we need to live victoriously in this life including His triumphant battle plan. When God presents a love opportunity, choose to take it and experience sight as Fruits of joy and peace burst forth.

Let's follow and finish the good work
God has prepared in advance for us.

BATTLE ORDERS
Ch 16 - Battle Like Jesus

TAKE AWAYS

1.

2.

3.

REFLECTION: Jesus' Triumphant Battle Plan Checklist: Are you following His example? On a scale of 1 to 5, rate your efforts.

_____ Seeking solitude with the Father often.

_____ Speaking the Word with authority against the enemy's accusations and lies in your life.

_____ Remaining in a posture of prayer and surrendering your will even when it's painful or doesn't make sense.

_____ Walking in obedience while receiving His grace covering when you fall short.

_____ Creating margin in your life so you notice divine appointments.

_____ Fulfilling love opportunities the Lord places in front of you.

Battle Action:

1. Write down any thoughts or feelings that come to mind as you read through this checklist. Receive conviction, and not

condemnation by casting out what is false and choosing right thinking.

2. What is God calling you to act on? How does He want you to respond?

BATTLE TOOL: Love (Activate your Greatest Weapon)

1. Turn your focus outward by looking for opportunities to be Jesus' hands and feet. Commit to at least one daily act of love for someone who you come in contact (i.e. encourage, compliment, pray for, serve, give, etc.)
2. Take a spiritual gifts assessment (via online or through your church) to determine your strengths. Where is God calling you to serve in love according to your gifts?
3. What (organizations) or who (groups or individuals) tugs at your heart? Research, pray and identify your passions. What next steps is God calling you to take toward those He has placed on your heart?

*Go deeper verses from the chapter: The Gospels - Matthew, Mark, Luke and John.

17

LOVE LIKE JESUS

A new commandment I give to you, that you love one another: just as I have loved you, you also are to love one another.

— John 13:34

2018 Mt Pleasant, SC

"Mommy, did you pack me a cookie for lunch?" my five-year-old inquired on the way to preschool.

I glanced back in my rearview mirror. "Not today baby, you had one before we left."

"But mom, I want a cookie." In an instant, Allie's beautiful smile turned into a tearful pout as her pleas continued to increase in octaves. It was pointless to try and make her understand why because she was no longer listening. She believed she was right and this "need" was of the utmost importance. Crying quickly turned into anger as she tried to force her will.

Twenty minutes later, we pulled into the school parking lot. I couldn't believe how this tantrum had escalated. I calmly unfastened her seatbelt, looked into her brown eyes full of distress and waited for them to meet mine. "I love you," I spoke as I firmly but gently stood my ground because I knew what was best. Suddenly, it was as if I was looking at myself in a mirror.

I understand Allie's frustration. So many times, I don't get what I want and then I'm the one kicking and screaming, demanding my way and falling into sin. Each time, my Heavenly Father patiently waits for me to turn my eyes back to Him as He whispers, "I love you."

God knows what is best and He will gently but firmly lead. Time and time again, I repeat my mistakes. Time and time again, He forgives and pours out His love anyway.

As my children grow and their sin gets bigger and more obvious, I ask God to help me respond to them with the same fierce, unconditional and compassionate love He bestows upon me. He's shown me that this act of love is meant to go well beyond the doors of my home. Nothing reflects Jesus more than when believers respond in love even to the worst of sinners.

While evil continues to impact our world, Jesus is calling us to be like Him and thus reciprocate. We are to pour out His fierce, unconditional and compassionate love onto others.

The Example

We are called to love God and others more than our self. This is being Kingdom-focused. Unfortunately, since mankind's naturally tendency is to focus inward, outward living does not come easy. As the enemy continues his deceptive tactics, we often become trapped and disarmed of our most powerful weapon, love.

I am called to look outward. That is what's best for me. So many times, I get so far into my head, that I cannot see what others are going through, nor can I find the energy to care. I simply can't get past what I'm going through. When this happens, I am held hostage to my feelings and my ability to battle severely weakens.

I have to remember my orders. They are not to strive harder and attain more. Nor are they to judge and point out imperfections in others. So many times, I overcomplicate my orders. Often, God is simply calling me to receive His love and mercy so that I can pour it out onto others.

We aren't just fighting for ourselves in this battle. We are fighting for all of God's children, especially the lost. The most powerful weapon we've been given to live victoriously and fulfill the great commission is love. To battle like Jesus, we have to learn how to love like Jesus. Just before His death, Jesus challenged His disciples by amending the greatest commandment.

A new commandment I give to you, that you love one another: just as I have loved you, you also are to love one another (John 13:34-35, emphasis mine).

There was no mistaking the timing of Jesus' words, for perfect love could not be fully known until His sacrifice was complete. The example had to be set. We are no longer called just to love one another as we would love ourselves, but instead to love as Jesus loved. Sacrificially. Unconditionally. Selflessly. Supernaturally!

In His final days, Jesus upped the stakes and left us His love example to follow.

HUMBLY SERVE OTHERS WITHOUT CONDITION

In John 13, at suppertime before Passover and hours before the greatest betrayal; Jesus took the lowly position of servant among His disciples. In a place where He was clearly the guest of honor, Jesus began to display love at a whole new level. Not only did He wash His followers' feet, He washed the feet of His earthly "enemy," or the one who would betray Him.

Jesus always served without expecting anything in return. Despite fully knowing Judas was about to hand Him over to die, Jesus chose to love him anyway. For years, He invited Judas to walk alongside Him and eat at His table. He treated Judas no different than the others. This incredible example of showing no favoritism, was and still is a powerful display of the Gospel.

INTERCEDE IN PRAYER FOR OTHERS, EVEN THOSE WHO OFFEND, HURT OR BETRAY

On the cross with the shame and sin of the world bearing down upon Him, Jesus looked out and saw mankind in its confused and deceived state:

- Roman officials who brutally tortured and mocked Him.
- Jewish leaders clouded by their pride and man-made rules.
- Followers ashamed because they had fled in fear.
- Followers spiritually blinded and grieving their Messiah.

Jesus interceded for each as He prayed Luke 23:34, *"Father, forgive them, for they know not what they do."* Spiritually, He knew the significance of what was happening and what was to come. As the final Passover Lamb completed His mission, forgiveness that transcends time was extended to all that would ever call upon Jesus as Lord.

LAY DOWN ONE'S LIFE FOR OTHERS

Jesus came to this world to die. Before His final moments of excruciating pain, He experienced every feeling humanity ever would. Not only was He taking on the transgressions of others, even the most of treacherous criminals; He was completely and perfectly innocent of any accusation. Jesus spent 33 years knowing what He had to do. Jesus chose to lay down His life for His friends, His "enemies" and ultimately His Father.

SEIZE EVERY OPPORTUNITY TO EDIFY AND RESTORE THE BROKEN

Before Jesus took His rightful place at the right hand of the Father, 1 Corinthians 15:6 states that He appeared separately to over 500 followers. Among the eyewitnesses was Peter, His loyal disciple who had fearfully denied knowing Him not once but three times. Peter had messed up big time, but no sin was too big for Jesus.

Jesus met Peter right where he was to reconcile and prepare him for his ultimate calling. In this encounter, Jesus asked Peter a simple question not once, but three times. *"Simon (Peter), son of John, do you love me?"* As Peter answered, *"You know I love you,"* our Redeemer responded with an if/then challenge each time (John 18:15-17):

1. *Feed my lamb*
2. *Tend my sheep*
3. *Feed my sheep*

Jesus lovingly revealed Truth and restored Peter, the rock whom He would build his church on. I believe with each question, Jesus was asking an underlying question to both prepare Peter for His future mission and spell out what it really means to love:

- Will you follow me and my example?
- Will you care for my people physically, emotionally and spiritually?
- Will you stand up for Truth no matter the cost?

Jesus is asking us the same question today. *Do you love me? If so, then:*

1. *Follow My lead*
2. *Walk in My example*
3. *Receive My power to fulfill what I call you to*

Love as I have loved

I have been crucified with Christ. It is no longer I who live, but Christ who lives in me. And the life I now live in the flesh I live by faith in the Son of God, who loved me and gave himself for me (Galatians 2:20).

True love, loving like Jesus, is only possible through *faith* in Jesus. When we commit our lives to Christ, the Holy Spirit comes in to dwell. This is what makes us capable of loving like Him. Trust Him in this process.

Jesus shows us how loving God and loving others is really one in the same. In Matthew 25:40 (NIV), Jesus says, *Whatever you did for one of the least of these brothers and sisters of mine, you did for me.* We love God by keeping His Word in our heart. And we love others by seeking to serve as Jesus did. When we serve and love others, we are actually serving and loving Christ.

While the Gospels use different terminology, the command on who to love is the same. Matthew writes we are to love other believers. John writes we are to love one another. And Mark writes we are to love our neighbor as He refers to the Law given to Moses.

It is not for us to know or decide God's chosen elect. We cannot see or judge the heart of another; therefore, we are to love and serve all without judgement.

God, help us become the neighbor, or good Samaritan, who shows mercy and compassion to all, especially when the enemy throws these deceptive arrows:

- *I'm too busy.*
- *I've got my own things to worry about.*
- *I just don't feel like it right now.*
- *They don't deserve it.*

The Home-less and the Love-less

Pure and genuine religion in the sight of God the Father means caring for orphans and widows in their distress and refusing to let the world corrupt you (James 1:27, NLT).

Let's break this verse down. The NIV translation reads real religion is *to keep oneself from being polluted by the world* (NIV). We do this by remembering, maintaining and applying the Word of God to our lives. These three behaviors equip and empower us to live out our calling, especially loving others.

The book of James is all about letting your actions speak what's in your heart. Since putting others first is not our natural tendency, we have to train our hearts by putting love into action instead of just talking about it. As we consistently pursue outward acts of love regardless of how we feel, our thinking will shift overtime to one of service. Now, the stage is set for Jesus to transform our hearts as well as others.

Real religion is also looking *after orphans and widows in their distress* (NIV). Does this verse mean we are just to tend to children without parents and wives without husbands? I don't believe so.

The *father-less* and the *husband-less*. The Merriam-Webster Dictionary defines an orphan as *one deprived of some protection or advantage*. The MSG translation of James 1:27 even reads we are to *reach out to the homeless and loveless in their plight*. We can't overlook these broader descriptions. This means our focus group just got bigger.

The *homeless* could really include anyone deprived or in distress. There are so many needs out there in the world today and they go well beyond the physical. For example, someone who is lonely is in need of interaction, support and understanding.

The *loveless* are simply those deprived of love. Some have been abandoned by loved ones, while others are just terribly hard to love. Since God is love, one could even translate the loveless to mean those without God.

Lesson Learned:
We can't judge the hearts and motives of others;
therefore, reach out and care for anyone God brings onto your path,
especially those who are hard to love.

The Hard to Love

"But to you who are listening I say: Love your enemies, do good to those who hate you, bless those who curse you, pray for those who mistreat you" (Luke 6:27-28, NIV).

Many overlook this group when implementing their love walk. This kind of sacrificial love is incredibly difficult; but when we ignore these opportunities, we are the ones being deceived and allowing the enemy to gain ground.

Think about it. The loveless are in need. They are in need of love. How did they get to this place of being hard to love? Hurting people normally are the ones who hurt others. They have received wounds. They have also been deceived. They are in need of someone to take a chance on them and be a testimony of God's grace and love in action. Loving to this degree is powerful and life-altering.

All God's chosen people should clothe themselves with compassion, not just the ones whose strengths and giftings are mercy. Additionally, we must show mercy to all people, not just to the ones we think deserve it.

Mercy is compassion and forgiveness put into action. It was done for us at the cross, therefore we are obligated to do unto others. If we do not, we are assuming God's place as judge. Christ lives in all of His people, and He loves all people. It's this same love that equips us to love others, even our "enemies."

Lesson Learned:
Step off the throne as judge and allow God His rightful place.

Radical love

And God is able to make all grace abound to you, so that having all sufficiency in all things at all times, you may abound in every good work (2 Corinthians 9:8).

Radical love goes beyond human wisdom and strength. It is desperately needed in this battle. Even nonbelievers show kindness to those they like. As Christians, how are we shining His light by doing the same?

Through Christ, we can "wash the feet" of our Judas'. We can pray for those who persecute us. We are capable of loving any who annoy, offend, betray and continually wound us. We can love radically just like Jesus if we choose to.

Radical love is a game changer!
It is mighty warfare against the kingdom of darkness,
and it's the last part of our winning strategy for a reason.

Radical love takes:

Spiritual lenses. What are we battling? Deception. Who is our real enemy? Satan, not man. What's really going on? Satan is attempting to manipulate our "hard to loves" for his purposes. Do not take the bait and be distracted by a physical enemy. Rather, go out of your way to serve them and watch what happens. As the saying goes, *kill them with kindness*, for they are not getting away with anything. Instead, you are preventing the enemy from his attempt to steal, kill and destroy.

God's overflow. We have to be so full of God's love that it spills out. It's not love unless it's from Him. If we are empty or barely filled, then how can we give out of an overflow? God is always pouring out His love to us. If we don't keep our lids open to receive, there will be no overflow and thus no radical love.

Putting love into action shifts our perspective and war efforts back onto the real enemy. Love, the greatest commandment, is our greatest weapon and when used radically will bring triumphant results!

Lesson Learned:
Radical love is letting God love through us.

Radical Forgiveness

Make allowance for each other's faults, and forgive anyone who offends you. Remember, the Lord forgave you, so you must forgive others (Colossians 3:13, NLT).

The hard truth is no matter what someone has done, we are called to forgive. Period. Why? Because through Christ's sacrifice, all sin was covered for those who belong to Him. God has forgiven us; therefore, we must forgive others. If we can't, we are removing God from the throne of our lives, taking His place as judge, and losing the daily battle. Trust Him to bring justice in your situation.

Do not take revenge, my dear friends, but leave room for God's wrath, for it is written: "It is mine to avenge; I will repay," says the Lord (Romans 12:19, NIV).

God is the judge and His justice is perfect. Holding onto and acting out in unforgiveness will never bring justice. Instead, it holds you captive, steals your spiritual fruit (thus the life and light within), weakens your testimony and can even make you physically ill. Oh, how we have been deceived!

Choosing to walk through the forgiveness process takes time. In fact, it's a daily choice. God will always meet us right where we are. If we ask, He will give us the *desire* to forgive. He will also provide the *power* to relinquish control and trust His justice. As we do, we are freed from our self-imposed prisons of bitterness. We begin to experience abundance through His joy and peace. Lives will be touched by the word of our testimony. Our health will even improve.

When I think of people who have expressed radical forgiveness, two extreme cases come to mind:

THE APOSTLE STEPHEN

He was a man full of faith and the Holy Spirit. In Acts, he found himself in a debate over Truth with some men of the Synagogue. Stephen was brought to the court on false charges of blasphemy, where he continued to boldly preach Christ is Lord. The Jewish leaders grew angry at his words and called for his stoning.

Stephen became the first martyr for Christ. His last words were very similar to Jesus'. Acts 7:59 reads, *And as they were stoning*

Stephen, he called out, "Lord Jesus, receive my spirit." And falling to his knees he cried out with a loud voice, "Lord, do not hold this sin against them." And when he had said this, he fell asleep. Despite the hatred and fatal blows, Stephen chose forgiveness as he kept His eyes on Christ and His Kingdom.

FAMILY MEMBERS OF A CHURCH MASS SHOOTING

In 2015, a shooter walked into an evening bible study at Mother Emmanuel AME Church (Charleston, SC), and gunned down nine believers. At the suspect's bond hearing, according to *Washington Post*, family members of the slain stood up one by one and declared their forgiveness towards the suspect. Despite the suspect's actions and lack of remorse, they chose and spoke radical forgiveness.

> *"I forgive you. You took something very precious from me. I will never talk to her again. I will never, ever hold her again. But I forgive you. And have mercy on your soul."*

> — NADINE COLLIER, FAMILY MEMBER

Imagine what occurred in the spiritual realm as these supernatural acts of love were on display for the public. Both stories were witnessed and recorded for the world to hear! This should inspire us. For it wasn't done in their own strength nor did they feel like forgiving.

Radical love takes supernatural strength. It is only through Christ that we are capable of supernatural love. Cast out the lie that *I can't forgive* and recognize the same power that raised Christ from the dead and the same power who gives strength to forgive lives in you.

While the martyr goes to be with Jesus, victims and their loved ones have to live with the repercussions of someone else's sin. There is a grief process, and part of it is daily battling the fleshly desire to hate and seek revenge. Forgiveness is a daily choice.

Notice the two examples above took a heart posture and outward action. Each spoke of their forgiveness, and I'm sure the victims still living have to speak "I forgive" aloud and often. Why? Because our hearts will follow what we hear, think on and believe.

Conclusion

Radical love is a huge blow to Satan and his kingdom:

- The enemy's distraction plan fails when we reject the "woe is me" perspective.
- The enemy's deception plan fails when the *Man (specific person) is my enemy* lie is exposed.
- God's supernatural grace is on full display when we extend mercy and forgiveness. This act results in a multitude of seed-planting opportunities.

Radical love, loving as Jesus loved, takes right perspective. No matter what we are facing, it's not about us. It's all about Him shining through us. Keep focused on God's Kingdom and your role in furthering it.

This world is not our home and there is *Someone* and *Something* much greater at work. In the scope of eternity, we are on this earth for only a blip of time, and our treasures are in heaven. With a Kingdom perspective, we are capable of loving no matter what obstacle or hurt we've experienced.

Showing mercy to others while in distress is counter cultural. Forgiving others is a choice our flesh wants no part of. Unfortunately, we will never feel like doing either, but we have been given all we need to carry it out anyway.

When we force our flesh to take proactive steps towards
love and forgiveness, our heart will follow.

TAKE AWAYS

1.

2.

3.

REFLECTION:

1. Read John 21:15-19 as if you are Peter. How is God calling you to:

- Care for His people spiritually and physically?
- Speak truth in fearful or tough circumstances?
- Obey no matter the cost?
- Love your "enemies"?

2. List 5 people (or types of people) who are *hard to love*. Do you have a Judas in your life? How can you show radical love to each?

BATTLE TOOL: Radical Love (Forgiveness)

- Who in your past or present has wounded, offended or betrayed you? Have you forgiven them?

- Have you offended someone and need to ask for forgiveness?
- Are you the one who you need to forgive?

God will meet you right where you are. Walk through the following forgiveness process with those God places on your heart.

1. Get mad at the real enemy, instead of your earthly offender.
2. Recognize Satan's plan to use raw and hurtful experiences to imprison with hurt and bitterness. Forgiving someone doesn't free your offender, it frees you!
3. Declare Philippians 2:13 "Lord, give me the desire and power to forgive!" (Repeat daily)
4. Pray for your offender daily. It is impossible to hate someone you are praying for.
5. Speak aloud – "*I forgive _____.*" (Repeat daily)
6. Meet with your offender, if God instructs you, and forgive face to face.
7. Move forward in freedom: Is God calling you to continue in a relationship with this person? Forgiveness doesn't necessarily mean reconciliation. There are many toxic relationships out there. Seek wise counsel about your specific situation.

*Go deeper verses from this chapters: John 18:15-27; John 21; Matthew 16:18.

18

REMAIN AND REMEMBER

It is for freedom that Christ has set us free. Stand firm, then, and do not let yourselves be burdened again by a yoke of slavery.

— GALATIANS 5:1, NIV

FALL 2015

I'd entered a new season with many roles: wife, mother, teacher, ministry leader and part-time direct salesperson. Nothing in me wanted to homeschool, but my gut was telling me to bring my kids back into the home for a year and train their hearts. My flesh put up a good fight, but deep down I knew this was about surrender. So, I looked past my feelings, put my big girl panties on and stepped out.

Since I was "obeying", God would make this easy, right?

As we all know, God's ways are often different from our own. He had some painful pruning to do. It was the hardest season I had faced in years. And, I can't even explain to you why, except that "performing" all my roles left me weary and defeated. It felt as if I was on a hamster wheel going many directions but getting nowhere.

I knew much of my struggle was wrong thinking and a cloudy perspective. I knew Satan was loving the discouragement, fatigue and anger I was allowing to stir within. Yet, I was too tired to stop the assaults and reopen my "lid". I began losing the daily battle and giving into destructive thinking. I became depleted – physically, emotionally and spiritually depleted.

In October, my kids and I traveled to Birmingham, AL to see my parents for the weekend. Meanwhile, a 1000-year flood event occurred back home and extended our stay. As I waited for the flood waters to recede, my children's behavior, or tolerance of it, rapidly declined. They had been running laps on my parent's beautiful hardwood floors for days dodging the antiques and decorative dishes displayed on the walls. When my grandparents came to visit for dinner, my kids couldn't sit still for two minutes or interact when spoken to. In that moment, I chose to stop fighting.

A variety of negatives ran through my mind: *I can't do this anymore. I'm a horrible mom. My kids are out of control. I'm such a... failure!* As soon as I allowed the "f" word space, that old song was set to repeat.

You're failing, you're failing, you're failing.

I am failing. With those three words, I had just agreed and surrendered, but unfortunately, to the wrong side. I am not proud of what followed. I allowed my old mental squatters of rejection, discouragement, depression and condemnation to return. I shut myself off from others, including God. I was mad at Him and didn't know what to do about it.

I couldn't escape from my prideful need to understand why. *Why was this happening? Why did I have to do this? Why is it not easier?*

I spiraled back into the old "pit" I said I'd never return to, being held captive to circumstance and a slave to wrong thinking. I let the TV raise my kids and ran from all responsibilities.

"Jesus, help me!" I cried out and Romans 8:28 came to mind:

God will bring all things together for good.

I pleaded for God to bring me back into His presence which I so desperately missed, and Psalm 139 came to mind:

I can never flee from your presence, for you are always there.

I prayed, "God, forgive me. Help me with my unbelief! What are you trying to show me?"

REMEMBER.

The word began to resonate from deep within. "Remember what?" I desperately begged.

REMAIN.

Then it hit me — I'd forgotten.

It is for freedom that Christ has set us free. Stand firm, then, and do not let yourselves be burdened again by a yoke of slavery (Galatians 5:1, NIV).

Stop and read this verse again.

You've just completed *The Believer's Battle Strategy*, and this is what Satan is banking on; you forgetting.

- *Forgetting* who you are, Whose you are and the power you possess.
- *Forgetting* the Truth and how to fight with Truth.
- *Forgetting* you are already and always will be free in Christ!

For some, it may seem impossible you could ever go back to *prison living*. Others are hopeful, as their arsenals are now filled and ready for battle. Eyes have been opened and God's Word has sparked a fire within. Some may even be boldly declaring "Hit me with your best shot!"

I was so sure I would never go back. Unfortunately, in my weakness, I took my eyes off of Christ, shut the lid to my heart and re-closed the painful places God had freed me from.

Lesson Learned:
Never discount your flesh, the noise of the world
and the adversary who waits for an opportune time.

Stay Alert

Jesus' Disciples say it best.

- Peter warns of our enemy, the devil, who prowls around looking for those who are not battle ready (1 Peter 5:8).
- Luke reminds us that just because we win the battle today doesn't mean Satan won't try again tomorrow (Luke 4:13).
- John gives us hard Truth, *in this world, we will have trouble* (John 16:33).

Just because we are Christians seeking God doesn't mean things will always be easy. In fact, the target on your back just got bigger. You are a threat because more of God's glory can be seen.

It's inevitable. Difficult seasons will come and threaten to deplete. Distraction and interference from circumstance, other people and mind-numbing arrows are just around the corner. There will be times when we forget and leave our battle tools at "camp." This fight goes well beyond boot camp. In fact, if we want to experience Christ and His promised abundance, fighting is our life's calling.

Do not grow weary, for the fight is not a curse. It's actually a hidden blessing, just like Paul's thorn. Thorns are painful but necessary. They are a reminder of our need for Christ. God craves our dependence on Him, so He can continue His good work in us. Self-sufficiency is utter deception. Without Christ, we are broken. This is why Christ came, to mend up the brokenhearted and bind up our wounds.

We are being transformed into His image, but this good work will not reach completion until Christ returns. Therefore, we are not "fixed" yet, we will not do everything right and we will sometimes forget. Never give up because you are now equipped. In moments of forgetfulness or weakness, do not receive condemnation. Instead, pick up your battle tools, put on your Power and follow orders.

Unwavering Belief

Truth never changes, but unfortunately, our belief in its power does. In order to experience the freedom, power and Truth we already possess; we have to first believe we have it. Just because someone calls them self a Christian doesn't mean they are, nor does it mean they automatically believe all God's promises. Faith muscles have to be strengthened.

What we think on is what we will eventually believe. Maintaining right focus is tough. Choosing to receive spiritual nourishment on those busy or "off" days is a test of perseverance. However, it is the key to remembering and remaining. When we choose to focus and dwell on things other than God, we forget Truth, our spirits weaken and our flesh seizes the opportunity to take over.

In those "civil war" moments of inner struggle,
will you choose to believe despite your feelings?

In those times you choose wrong, will you recognize,
repent and reclaim your God-given authority?

Believers, freedom is already ours! It occurred with an empty tomb that first Easter Sunday and can never be taken away. Do not become imprisoned again by wrong thinking, because that is all that can now enslave you. I repeat, choose write thinking. Truth thinking.

So much has been stolen from us based on what we will allow ourselves to think on and believe. This is why God wants us to not only mature in our walk, but also to have a child-like faith. It sounds like an oxymoron, but think about it. Children haven't yet been tainted by the world's ways, and they believe what their parents tell them.

Belief comes from meditating on or remaining in God's Word; our living, active and extraordinary weapon. God promises it will not return to Him void. What God says is. He calls us to believe His Word regardless of what we see, think or feel.

Lesson Learned:
Surrender and become like a child. He will increase in you!

Strategy Maintenance

As we complete *The Believer's Battle Strategy*, we have an important decision to make. Boot camp is over. We can either see this strategy as another "good read" and continue on with life as usual; or we can take the road less traveled, continue fighting like we've trained and not give up.

Fighting for the life Christ died to give you
is the narrow path. In fact, it's the only way to truly live.

There is no quick fix or "one and done" magic formula to victory living. It is a daily choice. If you root yourself in God's Word and apply it to your struggles, He will finish His good work and do the fighting for you.

I've tried my share of diets and "boot camp" workout regiments. What gets me is the maintenance part, once I get where I want to be. I often fall short because my strategy is either unsustainable or I choose to believe a quick fix with no lifestyle change is possible. Wrong thinking brings empty results. Short term solutions don't last. Sustained lifestyle change does.

Heart change is always needed for long-term results. A new lifestyle must be learned, applied and maintained; otherwise old habits and default thinking will return. Maintaining a posture of surrender to God and continuing the fight using your battle tools is strategy living. Leaning on God's power to fight, and not our own, is the solution.

> While it's not perfect living, it's abundant living
> in the midst of imperfection.

As you maintain your strategy, a funnel-like progression will result. The more you fight like you've trained, the more you will spiritually mature. The more you mature, the easier it will become and the shorter your detours will be. Continue to do your part and God will do His. It's a promise.

Lids open and Vessels full

> *But we have this treasure in jars of clay, to show that the surpassing power belongs to God and not to us* (2 Corinthians 4:7).

We are God's vessels, meant to be filled with His power and used for His purposes. God's plan is for His glory and love to be revealed and poured out into the world through us. Unfortunately, we are flawed, broken and often distracted. We cannot maintain or share our powerful contents without a constant flow from the Source. In fact, we will eventually run dry. Whatever we fill ourselves with will be what others see. Only when there is overflow can a vessel pour out.

- Choose to be filled with what is true, God's love and all-surpassing power.
- Keep your lids and broken places open to receive.
- Pour out His overflow onto others.

Come, all you who are thirsty, come to the waters. Jesus is pleading. He patiently waits to replenish His people with living water that never runs dry. When we feel weary, worried or depleted; our lids have closed. His living water recedes as we pour into our relationships and responsibilities.

Remember and remain. The words God gave me when I experienced temporary blindness back in 2015. He continues to show me how vital these concepts are for strategy maintenance.

Lesson Learned:
Remember to remain open for constant filling.

Remember Your Strategy

USE YOUR *WORD WEAPON.*
For the word of God is living and active, sharper than any two-edged sword, piercing to the division of soul and of spirit, of joints and of marrow, and discerning the thoughts and intentions of the heart (Hebrews 4:12).

PUT ON *GOD'S POWER.*
Finally, be strong in the Lord and in the strength of his might. Put

on the whole armor of God, that you may be able to stand against the schemes of the devil (Ephesians 6:10-11).

KEEP A *KINGDOM PERSPECTIVE.*
The kingdom of heaven is like treasure hidden in a field, which a man found and covered up. Then in his joy he goes and sells all that he has and buys that field (Matthew 13:44).

STAY CONNECTED WITH *BATTLE BUDDIES*, OR OTHER BELIEVERS.
Two are better than one...Though one may be overpowered, two can defend themselves. A cord of three strands is not quickly broken (Ecclesiastes 4:9,12, NIV).

RESET YOUR *MIND DEFAULT.*
You were taught, with regard to your former way of life, to put off your old self, which is being corrupted by its deceitful desires; to be made new in the attitude of your minds; and to put on the new self, created to be like God in true righteousness and holiness (Ephesians 4:22-24, NIV).

OPERATE USING YOUR *TRUTH FILTER.*
But the Helper, the Holy Spirit, whom the Father will send in my name, he will teach you all things and bring to your remembrance all that I have said to you (John 14:26).

TAKE *MENTAL INVENTORY.*
Behold, You desire truth in the innermost being, And in the hidden part [of my heart] You will make me know wisdom (Psalm 51:6, AMP).

EXERCISE YOUR *BATTLE TOOLS.*
Do not merely listen to the word, and so deceive yourselves. Do what it says (James 1:22, NIV).

There is so much to remember here.

If you're anything like me, the "to do" list is forming. Anxiousness takes over, reminding me of all the times I have, will and continue to forget. Weariness emerges because I "should" remember these things but often cannot. To my good intentions, Jesus sweetly whispers:

"Come to me, all you who are weary and burdened, and I will give you rest. Take my yoke upon you and learn from me, for I am gentle and humble in heart, and you will find rest for your souls. For my yoke is easy and my burden is light" (Matthew 11:28-30, NIV).

Jesus never called us to be perfect, He called us to persevere. Remembering is getting back on track when you recognize you're off the path.

Remain

Even on our best days, we cannot remember everything. Once again, we were never meant to be self-sufficient. That is why we were given the Holy Spirit, to teach and *remind* us of all things. But we have to be seeking and listening, or simply put *remaining,* for Him to do this. Therefore, our "to do" list really only comes down to one "do"; remain. For that is the only way to remember.

A bucket with holes needs constant filling from an independent source to remain full. Mankind is like a broken bucket. We can only be filled and free of brokenness by remaining focused on God, our Source. Otherwise, we become deserts of emptiness and self-destruction. To remain means to stay in a specific place or condition, unchanging. Our place is at the feet of Jesus in a posture fully dependent on Him.

We were created, by God and for God, to be His children whom He lavishly pours out His life onto. And when He does, the miraculous occurs. Jesus Christ, The Living Water, was sent to be our continuous life source and outpouring. Apart from Christ we are broken. *In Christ* we are complete, more than enough, and have everything we could ever need! The Holy Spirit was sent to remind and empower. When we remain, we are unstoppable!

REMAIN CONNECTED TO YOUR LIFE SOURCE.
Remain in me, as I also remain in you. No branch can bear fruit by itself; it must remain in the vine. Neither can you bear fruit unless you remain in me (John 15:4, NIV).

REMAIN VIGILANT AND ON GUARD, FOR THE BATTLE IS STILL RAGING.
Be alert and of sober mind. Your enemy the devil prowls around like a roaring lion looking for someone to devour (1 Peter 5:8, NIV).

REMAIN IN THE WORD, YOUR WEAPON.
"If you abide in my word, you are truly my disciples, and you will know the truth, and the truth will set you free" (John 8:31a-32).

REMAIN DEVOTED AND COMMITTED UNDER TRIALS.
Blessed is the man who remains steadfast under trial, for when he has stood the test he will receive the crown of life, which God has promised to those who love him (James 1:12).

The Battle is Won

The outcome of our daily battles depend on us. Think of your biggest battle, whether real or imagined. Now put it into perspective and learn from the Master!

In the midst of suffering on the cross, it looked as though Jesus had lost. Imagine being brutally beaten and murdered for show. Imagine being rejected by your closest friends. And if that wasn't enough, being abandoned by not only your father, but your Heavenly Father. As the enemy celebrated what physically looked like an impending victory, Jesus *chose* to stay focused spiritually.

Jesus trusted His death was His Father's will. He knew since the Father was allowing it, God in His sovereignty would use this tragedy for good. He trusted His pain was not for nothing. Believers, if there is any time to be more like Jesus, the time is now. For in this comes the fullness of the resurrection and an overflow of His abundance.

We are in Christ and *it is finished!* The war has already been won. Remember to remain in this Good News! We can trust that Christ in us knows all things and will carry us through any battle we face before He returns. Keep your Kingdom perspective and spiritual lenses on no matter what life brings, and you have also won: every – single – battle!

Fellow believers, *remember* to *remain*, stay alert
and continue to fight like you trained!

For everyone who has been born of God overcomes the world. And this is the victory that has overcome the world—our faith (1 John 5:4).

I'll see you out in the field!

ACKNOWLEDGMENTS

First, I want to thank my husband, George, and three children (Mason, Connor and Allie), who have all sacrificed much to make this book possible. George, you have sacrificed the most. You are my anchor who keeps me grounded and always supports or encourages me in what I set out to do. Thank you for believing in me! Mason, thank you for your artistic input on this project. I'm so proud of your talent and leadership abilities. Connor, thank you for always bringing sunshine to my day. Allie, thank you for being my side kick and cheerleader. I look forward to watching you all grow into who God created you to be.

My three cord strand, Lisa Bryant and Kathy Horn. Lisa, you were there in Togo 2012 at the very beginning of the BBS's conception and have been there ever since to encourage, challenge and spur me on every day. Thank you for being my Barnabas and for the impact you have made on my life! Kathy Horn, my Paul. You have taught me so much especially how to be a willing vessel for the Lord. Thank you for being such an impactful friend and mentor!

Thank you to my home church, Seacoast Church, for providing me with an opportunity to step out with God into this calling. Specifically Julie Hiott, thank you for believing in and trusting me to develop this ministry. Your wisdom, encouragement and insight throughout this process is not overlooked.

To the hundreds of ladies who have participated in the Battles to Breakthroughs Course since 2012, thank you for taking a chance on this class and aiding the development of it. Thank you to the 30 (and counting) ladies who answered the call to be a part of the Battles team over the years. Your friendship, insight, time and efforts are some of my most precious treasures. I humbly thank God for each you.

Shawn McCarthy, thank you for being a friend and inspiration. Thank you for both recognizing how the Battles message crosses genders, and stepping out to bring it to the men at Seacoast Church. Thank you, Anna, for being an intricate part in this and my team. Thank you to all the men who have participated in the Battles course. May the message continue to spread to all believers, both men and women.

My friend, Marney McNall, who not only served on the Battles Team but also sacrificed her time sharing her writing and editing expertise for this manuscript. She has taught me so much and I will be forever grateful!

Thank you Abbey Carmon, my graphic designer, for your selfless time and effort on this project. I love how God works in mysterious ways and brings people into each other's lives. I'm thankful for our friendship and look forward to seeing where God takes you.

Christian authors, specifically Joyce Meyer (Battlefield of the Mind), John Eldridge (Waking the Dead) and Neil Anderson (The Bondage Breaker) whose messages aided tremendously in my spiritual growth and the inspiration of this book.

I thank God everyday for what He has done and will continue to do. This book is for His glory alone. May I not take a single piece of it.

CHRISTIE PUNCH MICHAUD

https://www.believersbattlestrategy.com
Visit my website and subscribe to my newsletter for updates,
upcoming course opportunities and information on how to bring
the BBS to your local church.

Follow my blog for strategy living techniques.
https://blog.believersbattlestrategy.com

Made in the USA
Columbia, SC
15 July 2019